Art and Ethnicity

The Ukrainian Tradition in Canada

Canadian Museum of Civilization

Canadian Cataloguing in Publication Data

Main entry under title:

Art and ethnicity: the Ukrainian tradition in Canada

Issued also in French under title: Art et ethnicité.
"The essays contained in the book are meant to provide an informative backdrop to the exhibition." [held at the Canadian Museum of Civilization]
Includes bibliographical references.
ISBN 0-660-12910-8

1. Art, Ukrainian — Canada — Exhibitions. 2. Ethnic art — Canada — Exhibitions. 3. Ukrainians — Canada — History — Exhibitions. 4. Ukrainians — Canada — Social life and customs — Exhibitions. 5. Ukrainians — Canada — Ethnic identity — Exhibitions. I. Canadian Museum of Civilization. II. Title: The Ukrainian tradition in Canada

FC106.U5A77 1991 971.'00491791 C91-098558-8
F1035.U5A77 1991

NM 98-3/70-1991E

Édition française : *Art et Ethnicité — La tradition ukrainienne au Canada*

Published by:
Canadian Museum of Civilization
100 Laurier Street
P.O. Box 3100, Station B
Hull, Quebec
J8X 4H2

Printed in Canada

Canada

Credits

General Editor: Robert B. Klymasz
Managing Editor/Text Editor: Catherine Carmody
Designer/Production Officer: Deborah Brownrigg
Desktop Publishing: Francine Boucher
Photographs of artworks and objects: Harry Foster

The artifacts that illustrate this publication are from the collection of the Canadian Centre for Folk Culture Studies (CCFCS), Canadian Museum of Civilization. The historical/ethnographic photographs (except for front cover and page 26) are from CCFCS's Documents Collection.

Cover illustrations: (*Front*) Ukrainian immigrants from Galicia arrive in Canada, c. 1900 (National Archives of Canada C-5611); colour insets: *bandura*, 1962, wood with metal strings, made in Grimsby, Ont., 140.0 x 48.8 x 9.0 cm (CCFCS 75-1366); *Dancing Couple* c. 1973, carved and painted softwood, wall plaque by Stefan Pidsosny, 1906–1977, 18.4 x 11.5 x 2.5 cm (CCFCS 73-979). (*Back*) Picture frame, c. 1970, carved and painted birchwood, by Steven Petelycky, b. 1923, 33.5 x 29.0 cm (CCFCS 72-725).

The Canadian Museum of Civilization gratefully acknowledges the following for permission to use excerpts from their works: p 19, McClelland and Stewart Ltd., for the English translation of the Roy quotation, from *The Fragile Lights of Earth: Articles and Memories, 1942–1970*, 1982; p. 25, McClelland and Stewart Ltd.; p. 37, Janice Kulyk Keefer; p. 68 Maara Lazechko Haas, first published in the Canadian Authors Association's *Spirit of Canada*, 1977; p. 70, © Straight Arrow Publishers, from *Rolling Stone*, 15 June 1989. The epigraph on p. 51 is from a letter (Kurelek to Klymasz) in the CCFCS's Documents Collection; the one on p. 39 is from a report by Miriam Elston about an Easter service in a Ukrainian church, published in *Onward*, Toronto, 1916.

Contents

FOREWORD

As Governor General of Canada, I am delighted to have this opportunity to join with the Canadian Museum of Civilization in saluting the centenary of Ukrainian settlement in Canada (1891–1991). With its focus on artistic expression as a fundamental aspect of Canada's Ukrainian heritage, the exhibition **Art and Ethnicity: The Ukrainian Tradition in Canada** underlines the significance of our country's multicultural resources and the enrichment these bring to all Canadians.

This publication, a companion volume to the exhibition, complements the works on display and offers a variety of insights into an experience that is especially meaningful for readers of Ukrainian descent. However, others can also celebrate this particular facet of Canada's cultural make-up. Together we can all indulge in the colour, verve and fascination of a tradition that ranges from mystical icons to intricate needlework. Moreover, collectively we can take pride in ourselves, our nation and its institutions for preserving and fostering traditions that can appeal to everyone.

As I am a descendant of Ukrainian immigrants to Canada, this centenary marks an auspicious moment in my tenure of office as Governor General of Canada. It is customary for Ukrainians to celebrate special occasions like this with joyful exclamations of *"mnohaya leeta!"* ("many more years ahead"); within the present historical context, it is an expression that aptly reflects my own good wishes for Canada's Ukrainian legacy.

Ramon J. Hnatyshyn

Curator's Statement

This book grew out of the exhibition **Art and Ethnicity: The Ukrainian Tradition in Canada**. The exhibition was organized by the Canadian Museum of Civilization to salute the Ukrainian-Canadian centenary (1891–1991). The essays contained in the book are meant to provide an informative backdrop to the exhibition. Individually they constitute descriptive or interpretive statements on the history, experiences, folk arts, religious iconography and related art works of Ukrainians in Canada. Together they suggest a variety of approaches to understanding the subject matter in the exhibition.

Art and Ethnicity, the exhibition, represents several years of research and documentation amassed by the Museum's Canadian Centre for Folk Culture Studies. The approach to the exhibition began to crystallize in 1988 when our work pointed to a predilection among contemporary Ukrainian Canadians for artwork to express many facets of their ethnic heritage. Concomitantly, it was noted that such expressions of ethnicity were not necessarily always produced by professionals or by artists of Ukrainian descent. The exhibition offered an ideal vehicle for furthering our appreciation of the ethnic factor in Canadian art and related cultural phenomena. From a wider perspective, curatorial preparations for **Art and Ethnicity** seemed to coincide with trends and investigative concerns in other countries of the world, as exemplified by the scholarly symposia "Ethnological Picture Research" (Stockholm, 1986), "Cultural Differentiation and Cultural Identity in the Visual Arts" (Washington, D.C., 1987) and "Traditions of Expressive Folk Culture in Contemporary Art" (Moscow, 1988).

The link between art and ethnicity suggested by the Ukrainian tradition in Canada awaits further attention since it is evident that Canada's multicultural heritage finds in art an important vehicle and outlet for its expression. In this connection, the most productive formulation appears to be two-dimensional art, which, by a process of framing and compression, serves as a filter highlighting those elements of the legacy that continue to inspire, provoke and entertain.

It is almost impossible to cite and credit by name all those who have helped and collaborated in the process of mounting **Art and Ethnicity**. The support of donors and lenders to the exhibition was indispensable. The gift of two large collections in particular was critical in realizing the exhibition: one from the Ukrainian Heritage Association and Museum of Canada, Toronto; the other from Doris E. Yanda, Edmonton, which is now called The Doris (Daria) E. Yanda Ukrainian Collection. Three individuals deserve special thanks for their expertise in surveying communities in various parts of the country: Louise Binette (Montréal), Elizabeth Beaton (Sydney, Nova Scotia) and Olya Marko (Winnipeg). A final note of appreciation is extended to colleagues and co-workers at the Canadian Museum of Civilization: their talents and attentiveness contributed much to making this project a meaningful and rewarding museological experience.

Robert B. Klymasz
Curator, East European Programme

Art and Ethnicity

Frances Swyripa

From Sheepskin Coat to Blue Jeans:

A Brief History of Ukrainians in Canada

Ukrainian-Canadian history officially began on 7 September 1891 when Ivan Pylypiw and Vasyl Eleniak, peasants from the village of Nebyliv in Galicia, western Ukraine, stepped off the SS *Oregon* onto Quebec soil. The two men had come to the new Dominion of Canada to investigate rumours of "free land" in the West. Their reports were favourable, generating an excitement among their land-hungry fellow citizens that launched one of the largest immigrations Canada has seen. Of course, beginnings are rarely this precise, and Pylypiw and Eleniak were most certainly not the first Ukrainians to set foot in the country. Tradition, backed by inconclusive evidence, points to earlier arrivals who participated in Russian exploration on the Pacific coast, fought with the de Meuron regiment in the War of 1812 and accompanied the Mennonites to Manitoba in the 1870s. But such individuals, isolated and shadowy figures, established no identifiable or permanent Ukrainian presence. They play a symbolic role, in that they represent "roots" and allow Ukrainian Canadians to lay claim to a greater portion of Canada's past, but as founders they cannot compete with Pylypiw and Eleniak.

These two men did not inaugurate the mass movement of Ukrainians to Canada alone. In 1895, a member of the Galician intelligentsia, Dr. Josef Oleskiw, also toured Canada to determine its suitability for impoverished Ukrainian peasants, and he approached Canadian government officials about the possibility of large-scale assisted immigration schemes. Although the Canadian response was not enthusiastic, Oleskiw stimulated widespread interest in Canada in his native Galicia, and in Ukrainian-Canadian mythology he

(opposite page)

A family in western Ukraine poses just before emigrating to Canada, the land of opportunity, circa 1904.

Gift of the Ukrainian Heritage Association and Museum of Canada, Toronto

Leave them alone and pretty soon the Ukrainians will think they won the battle of Trafalgar.

— Stephen B. Leacock, *My Discovery of the West,* 1937

completes the triumverate of "founding fathers." Even then, Ukrainian immigration might not have reached the proportions it did had not Clifford Sifton, in 1896, become Minister of the Interior responsible for immigration in Sir Wilfrid Laurier's Liberal cabinet. His immigration policies, tapping non-traditional sources in central and eastern Europe for agriculturists capable of withstanding the rigours of pioneering in the western interior, permanently altered the complexion of Canada. Thrown into the French-English equation was a third, as of then, unknown quantity. Politicians and the public, looking askance at the newcomers' cultural baggage and often low standard of living, debated their impact on the national fabric. Sifton defended his actions with the now famous statement: "I think a stalwart peasant in a sheepskin coat, born on the soil, whose forefathers have been farmers for ten generations, with a stout wife and a half dozen children, is good quality." Others were less convinced, labelled them "Sifton's pets"—dirty, ignorant and garlic smelling—and demanded their assimilation to British-Canadian ideals and standards of conduct.

By the outbreak of the Great War in 1914, some 170,000 Ukrainian peasants seeking a fresh start overseas had made Canada their home. They came as members of a subjugated nation, ruled by Imperial Russia (larger eastern Ukraine)

Nicholas Pesklivets, 1911–1988
The Old Homestead 1987

Oil on canvas
40.5 x 30.5 cm

CCFCS 88-177

Shelagh Miller, 1928–
Church at Toutes Aides circa 1987

Watercolour
56.5 x 41.2 cm

CCFCS 88-162

and the Austro-Hungarian Empire (which controlled the western provinces of Galicia, Bukovyna and Transcarpathia). Austria-Hungary supplied the great majority of immigrants to Canada, with Galicia the principal source, Bukovyna a distant second. Most of the new arrivals went to homesteads in Manitoba, Saskatchewan and Alberta, so that in 1911, 94 per cent of Ukrainians in Canada lived in the prairie provinces. There they shunned the open prairie for the parkland, forming a series of bloc settlements that stretched in an arc from southeastern Manitoba to just east of Edmonton. As kin, fellow villagers, and simply people from the same district sought each other out, they created distinct pockets that reflected the settlers' desire for continuity and familiarity.

Within the bloc settlements, a way of life developed that lay outside that of the dominant Anglo-Canadian culture. Until the interwar years, the railway towns springing up along the newly laid tracks that crossed the blocs remained largely alien places. Instead, Ukrainian immigrants bought basic supplies, mailed and received letters, and went to school at rural crossroads communities where their own kind prevailed. Here, too, they attended their distinctive onion-domed churches—Greek Catholic if from Galicia, Orthodox if from Bukovyna—and participated in the cultural-educational clubs and ideological organizations that were patterned on old-country models and reflected old-country politics. These Ukrainian institutions dominated formal community and social life, just as informal socializing involved other Ukrainians, and both helped sometimes disoriented and anxious immigrants to adapt to their new surroundings.

Also crossing the ocean were Ukrainian peasant traditions and practices and a material culture whose impact was felt in the farming operations, in the home and in the ritual observances marking the seasons and life's major passages. Accustomed to a mean and frugal existence, Ukrainians initially homesteaded with the simple tools and outdated methods of their ancestors, producing largely for their own subsistence. Living conditions bore testimony to their poverty, to the demands of pioneering and to lack of acquaintance with the technological and scientific advances of the industrial age. While other women on the frontier, for example, had to learn to do without sewing machines and mass-produced, store-bought bread, Ukrainian immigrant peasant women had yet to discover that such wonders existed. To the shock of those who nurtured a vision of delicate and sheltered womanhood, Ukrainian pioneer women also worked on the land. While a function of poverty and the peasant family as a socio-economic unit, such labour was equated with the treatment of women as "beasts of burden and domestic drudges" and seen as proof of Ukrainian inferiority.

Immigrating to Canada to escape the deficiencies of a system responsible for unprofitable farming, widespread illiteracy and an unenviable standard of living, Ukrainian immigrants and their leaders soon rejected aspects of their way of life that were synonymous with "peasantness" and antithetical to "progress." By the 1920s, farmers were moving out of subsistence into mechanized and commercial agriculture. Although most of the profits went into tractors and binders for the field, some went into labour-saving devices for the home like cream separators and washing machines, and "luxury" items like the telephone and radio. And although some farm families grumbled that school deprived them of a pair of hands, or was unnecessary for girls destined to be housewives, others saw education as the key to upward mobility.

Modernization ultimately made alienation from the worldview that had governed the Ukrainian peasants' actions and psyche inevitable. Natural cycles, the spirit world, superstition and pagan agricultural rituals grafted onto those of the church had determined the rhythms of peasant life in the old country. But as education and science invaded the bloc settlements, it became increasingly difficult, for example, to believe in the efficacy of sympathetic magic—that the greater the number of times a peasant wife wound her scarf around her head, the fatter the heads of cabbage she grew in her garden.

Some rituals were retained, although their original meaning was gradually lost as the immigrants' descendants became ever removed from their peasant origins and agricultural roots. Traditionally, a special sheaf of wheat, or *didukh*, believed to contain the souls of dead ancestors, was saved from the harvest; brought into the house on Christmas Eve, it was returned to the field on New Year's Eve and burned to reunite the souls with the soil. Today, a largely ceremonial *didukh* has been transformed into a symbol of Ukrainian identity and consciousness. Ukrainian folk dances, songs and handicrafts also made the journey to Canada. Although becoming increasingly formalized and marginal to daily life, they too survived, so that folk dances and handicrafts, together with Ukrainian foods, have become major symbols of Ukrainian-Canadian identity.

William Kurelek, 1927–1977
In Our Own Family circa 1974

Lithograph
45.0 x 33.4 cm

The table is set for the traditional feast of meatless foods on Ukrainian Christmas Eve.

CCFCS 75-1301

Not all Ukrainians went to homesteads in western Canada, and not all homesteaders immediately became full-time farmers, as the need for cash forced many to seek temporary outside employment. At the lowly end of an ethnic hierarchy in the workplace, male wage earners laboured on railway gangs, in the mines, in logging camps and on construction sites, performing the unskilled tasks of physical nation building. Many Ukrainian girls and young women also worked for wages, either to supplement the family income or because they had immigrated alone and had to earn their own living. With as few skills to offer as their male counterparts, they became waitresses, hotel chambermaids, maids in private homes and factory workers. While male workers were to be found on remote resource frontiers as well as in Canada's cities, and comprised a transient group, female workers were an urban phenomenon and relatively immobile.

The single and unattached developed their own subculture as they coped with an often unsympathetic boss or mistress, the isolation and boredom of camp life and the confines of a crowded boardinghouse or live-in service. Ukrainian and Anglo-Canadian leaders alike criticized their choices and priorities—the men for their fondness for the tavern and pool hall, girls and young women for their hats, chewing gum and face powder. Ukrainian leaders also chastised the latter for the gravest sin of all, shame of their origins as they sought status and acceptance in the Anglo-Canadian world through English husbands.

Before emigrating to Canada in 1938 this determined-looking Ukrainian woman dressed in all her finery for this studio portrait. The entire costume, made circa 1930, was acquired by the Canadian Museum of Civilization. The colour inset provides a closer view of her fine embroidery work.

CMC 75-13085 (woman)
CCFCS 75-1165 (inset)

Joining the pioneer urban working class was a small number of Ukrainian businessmen drawing their clientele from their fellow Ukrainians. Along with the men and women trained as teachers for the bloc settlements, these pioneer businessmen formed the core of what was to become the Ukrainian-Canadian middle class.

As in rural areas, Ukrainian immigrants settling in urban centres tended to congregate together. In the poorer sections of the city core, like Winnipeg's famous North End, in what came to be called the "foreign ghetto," they lived in tenement housing and erected their churches and halls. Today, many of these buildings still stand, visible symbols of a Ukrainian-Canadian community and organizational life. Some perform their original functions; others have been sold as Ukrainians prospered and moved out of the inner-city immigrant reception area. The gateway to the West, and soon surrounded by a rich hinterland in the Ukrainian bloc settlements of Manitoba, Winnipeg outstripped all rivals in attracting Ukrainian immigrants. The city's North End became the focal point of Ukrainian activity, enjoying its pre-eminence in community affairs until challenged by Toronto and Edmonton after the Second World War.

Two subsequent immigrations augmented the pioneer base. Some 68,000 Ukrainians, again primarily peasants from western Ukrainian territories, arrived between the wars. Although destined like their predecessors for prairie farms, they also contributed to the growth of Ukrainian urban communities, most notably in Ontario. Another 35,000 Ukrainians came to Canada in the wake of the Second World War. "Displaced persons" forcibly removed to western Europe as Nazi slave labour, they refused repatriation to the Soviet Union (which had annexed western Ukraine) at the war's end. From interwar Soviet as well as non-Soviet territories, generally better educated and more diverse than the two earlier immigrations, the new arrivals preferred central Canada over the Prairies, urban life over rural. Almost one-half went to Ontario, where they favoured the southern peninsula over the resource centres of the north and west, and one-fifth to Quebec.

The displaced persons, who injected a new dimension into the group profile without altering its basic character, were the last Ukrainians to come to Canada in significant numbers. Limited emigration from Poland and the Soviet Union since the 1970s has brought a trickle of newcomers,

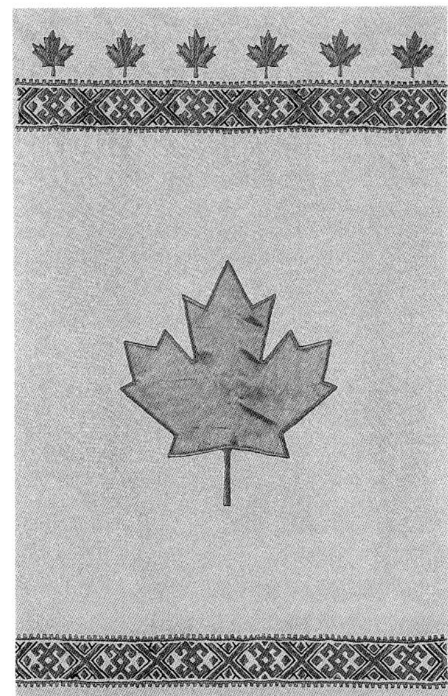

This detail is from a ritual towel used as a prop by Ukrainian performers from Winnipeg, Manitoba, during their concert tour of Ukraine in 1986. The maple leaf design and the traditional embroidery motif symbolize two legacies — Canadian and Ukrainian.

200 x 27 cm (towel)
approx. 65 x 27 cm (detail)
Gift of Myron Shatulsky, Winnipeg, Manitoba

CCFCS 89-5

Feelings of isolation and estrangement among Ukrainian settlers on the Prairies were alleviated by parish feast days. At such times, the community gathered to socialize, as depicted here, in Ethelbert, Manitoba, 12 July 1930.

CMC 85-3627

and a few immigrants arrive annually from other countries. Today Ukrainian Canadians are overwhelmingly Canadian born.

Immigration and natural increase had combined to make Ukrainian Canadians the fourth largest ethnic group in Canada in 1941, forming 2.7 per cent of the population. They were surpassed by the British, the French and the Germans. By 1981, when 529,615 Canadians gave "Ukrainian" as their origin on the census form, Ukrainian Canadians had fallen to fifth place, supplanted by the Italians. The peasant pioneer base in the prairie provinces has been eroded, both by the gravitation of the third immigration to central Canada and by interprovincial migration as Ukrainian Canadians joined other westerners attracted to industrial Ontario and neighbouring British Columbia. Yet the peasant pioneer base still makes itself very much felt. In 1981, 58.4 per cent of Ukrainian Canadians still lived on the Prairies; 25.3 per cent resided in Ontario, 12.0 per cent in British Columbia, 2.8 per cent in Quebec, and 0.5 per cent in Atlantic Canada.

Despite disagreement over the meaning of the terms, Ukrainian Canadians today are both "Canadian" and "Ukrainian." The persistence, peculiar nature and indeed crystallization of Ukrainian-Canadian identity or ethnicity rests on two factors. One is the group experience in Canada, the other the fate of twentieth-century Ukraine.

The timing of the first and largest wave of immigration was significant in the shaping of Ukrainians' Canadian consciousness. Late nineteenth- and early twentieth-century

Canada was in the throes of physical and psychological nation building. The country needed workers to exploit its resources, build its cities and railways, and open the West to agricultural settlement. A populous and productive West, propagandists argued in particular, was the key to national greatness, with Canada perhaps even replacing the mother country, Great Britain, as the heart of the empire. At the same time, Canada was to be a British country, erected on the values and institutions of its Anglo-Canadian element. In the period of settlement it was precisely because they were participants in the endeavour that would spell national success or failure that Ukrainians were subjected to such scrutiny and made the specific target of assimilation programs. The special attention they received acknowledged three interlocking factors: their large numbers, their concentration in the prairie provinces in bloc settlements and an escalating group identity. All the above factors have had a great impact on how Ukrainian Canadians perceive themselves as part of the Canadian experience.

In the legacy of the peasant pioneers, symbolized by Pylypiw and Eleniak, lies Ukrainian Canadians' birthright as Canadians. Their backbreaking toil and sacrifice to introduce ten million acres of virgin soil to the plough, and to exploit mining and forest frontiers so that Canada could be great, made Ukrainian Canadians founding peoples, especially of western Canada. To adherents of the peasant pioneer myth, it is also important that Ukrainians were preceded in Canada by a grain of wheat from their native Galicia; ancestor of the early maturing Red Fife, this seed was what made large-scale wheat production on the Prairies feasible. For their part, the peasant pioneers brought their love of the soil, a tremendous capacity for work and courageous perseverance; they laboured without government assistance, with meagre resources on often submarginal lands and in the face of prejudice and discrimination from the host society. Theirs is the story of progress and success, subsequently extended to all walks of life.

There is little doubt that Ukrainian Canadians have a definite sense of themselves and feel strongly about it. The tradition of the crucial Ukrainian role in providing the work force for early twentieth-century Canadian growth, and subsequent participation in all aspects of Canadian development, is not just the self-serving propaganda of an intellectual and economic elite but captures a genuine grassroots sentiment.

The Ukrainian population in Canada...is no longer tied to the land. It is no longer even a minority in the strict sense of the word. It is too involved in our national life, it has participated too intimately in Canada's self-expression to merit this description....Its traditions have passed into our national heritage.

—Gabrielle Roy, 1943

William Stefanchuk
Tilling the Soil circa 1945

Carved and painted wood
82 x 30 x 21 cm

CCFCS 75-2

Ukrainian Canadians' sense of belonging and participation in Canadian nation building through the peasant pioneers has embraced all generations and immigrations. In some respects, however, the peasant pioneer myth appeals most to those with western Canadian roots, and it cannot be separated from the broader western Canadian scene in which it is rooted. The decades since 1945 have witnessed a large-scale popular romanticization of the homesteading era in the prairie provinces and of the men and women challenged to superhuman feats. It is a nostalgic escape from an increasingly complex world, in which the significance of rural prairie communities and their residents has been eroded, to a simpler time when the West figured prominently in the scheme of things and westerners were perceived to be in command of their fates. That the proliferating local histories, which are a product of this phenomenon, transcend the pioneer generation to include the newest babe in arms testifies to the importance of continuity and place among the pioneers' descendants and the need for westerners to reaffirm themselves in the present. The participation of Ukrainian Canadians in these processes reflects experiences and convictions shared as westerners with groups of other ethnic origins. In rooting their demands for due recognition as Canadians in their role in opening the West, Ukrainian

Canadians emphasize the assimilative dimension of their experience. It focuses on a traditional theme of national development and highlights events in which Ukrainians have participated in common with other Canadians. Growing willingness on the part of the mainstream to give Ukrainian Canadians their wanted recognition in building the West, and through it the nation, has paralleled public acceptance of the idea of Canada as a "mosaic" or multicultural nation.

Mainstream legitimization of the Ukrainian Canadian experience through its pioneer and progress myths has many expressions. An Edmonton road, for example, bears the name Eleniak, an Edmonton park Oleskiw. William Kurelek has been elevated to an "all-Canadian" artist, his paintings of Ukrainian prairie homesteads regarded as a reflection of Canada in a manner reminiscent of the Group of Seven. Historian Ramsay Cook has said of Kurelek that "one of the great achievements of his art [in depicting the settling of the land] was that it gave recognition to the part Ukrainian Canadians played, their sacrifices and their achievements."* Similarly, in Pierre Berton's popular history of the settlement of the West, *The Promised Land*, Ukrainians move to the centre of the national epic as the book opens with Joseph Oleskiw and his dream for Galician peasants on the Canadian frontier.

"Canadianism" represents one side of the hyphen. Pivotal to the evolution of *Ukrainian* consciousness in Canada, colouring Ukrainian Canadians' attitudes to their homeland and heritage, is the fact that Ukrainian immigration occurred at a critical juncture not only in Canadian but also in Ukrainian nation building. Echoing contemporary developments among other Slavic peoples, the late nineteenth century witnessed the national awakening of the Ukrainian peasant mass. When the Russian and Austro-Hungarian empires crumbled in 1917–18, Ukrainians translated this new sense of "peoplehood" into a bid for political independence. The Ukrainian People's Republic, however, proved unable to withstand Soviet and Polish aggression or to influence world leaders redrawing the map of Europe. By the early 1920s, western Ukraine had been divided among the new states of Poland, Romania and Czechoslovakia, while the bulk of eastern Ukraine was incorporated into the Soviet Union as the Ukrainian Soviet Socialist Republic. The

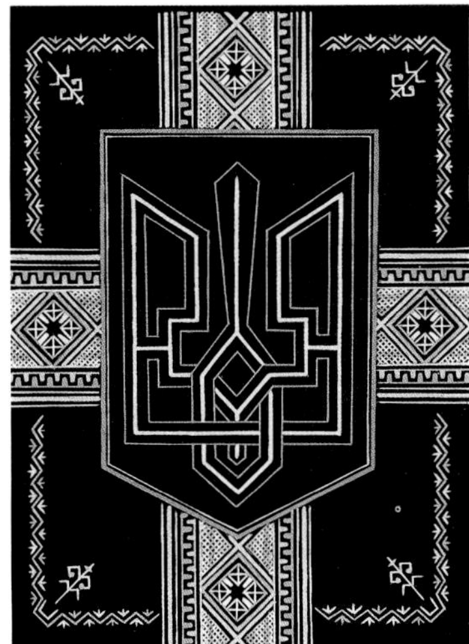

Steven Petelycky, 1923–
Wall plaque with multicoloured trident design and motifs imitating embroidery, circa 1970.

Carved and painted birchwood
28 x 21 cm
Gift of the artist

The trident has long served as a symbol of Ukraine's national aspirations.

CCFCS 72-724

*Fuller source citations can be found in the Selected Readings and Works Cited section.

Memorabilia relating to Ukraine's brief period of national independence as a free state (1917–1920) include postage stamps and money bills, which were often designed by leading artists of the time. The trident and figures in traditional dress were among the favourite symbols used.

CCFCS 89-613 (stamp)
CCFCS 89-603 (money bill)

suppression of national-cultural life, coupled with intellectual purges and artificial famine in Soviet Ukraine, threatened Ukrainian community life and physical survival itself. The Second World War brought further hardship under Soviet and Nazi occupations and another aborted bid for independence. After 1945 the Soviet regime continued to subject Ukraine to centralization through Moscow, and persisted in its policies of Russification, the suppression of dissent and human rights, and censorship of national-cultural life.

The unfinished business of Ukrainian nation building has had a profound impact on the course and content of Ukrainian consciousness in Canada. Leaving their homeland when Ukrainian identity was still being formed, turn-of-the-century peasant immigrants were "Ukrainianized" in Canada as much as in Ukraine; for many, despite the best efforts of community leaders, their Ukrainian consciousness remained more passive than active, more cultural than political. But interwar and postwar immigrants brought an often intense nationalism together with bitter ideological differences that stimulated both the coalescence and factionalization of Ukrainian-Canadian community life. With the exception of a pro-Soviet minority, the organized community has been united in support of an independent, non-Communist Ukrainian state, although disagreements on the nature of the future Ukrainian state and Ukrainian-Canadian involvement in its realization have frequently hindered cooperation for the greater and common good. Moreover, the organized community has argued that persecution of the Ukrainian language and culture in Ukraine, its subjugation to the Soviet political regime and the resulting unnatural relationship of Ukrainian Canadians with their homeland have made survival in Canada imperative.

Regardless of how many Ukrainian Canadians share the concerns of the community elite, the goals of this elite have been projected as the vision uniting and animating the masses. The idea that commitment to Ukraine and to national-cultural survival is not only necessary but also the duty of Ukrainians living in a land of freedom and socio-economic opportunity implies that group membership and its obligations are involuntary. It also puts Ukrainian Canadians in the forefront of a political lobby for an official multiculturalism policy to service their special needs.

It is to promote this ethnic pluralism, as much as to ensure acceptance in Canadian society, that Ukrainian Canadians emphasize their role in the development of the country. As Canadians who are full partners in Confederation—earned through their physical role in nation building as a founding people of western Canada, blood sacrifice in two world wars and enrichment of Canadian life in all spheres—many Ukrainians feel that they have the right to make political and financial demands on the state on behalf of their group.

Reflecting Ukrainians' numerical and therefore political strength, as well as the pluralistic nature of western society, the prairie provinces have been the most receptive to the Ukrainian community's lobby for the government-funded language and education programmes considered crucial to survival. As a result of Ukrainian initiative in the 1970s, first Alberta and then Manitoba and Saskatchewan approved bilingual instruction in English and any other language in their respective school systems. Today, a few thousand pupils from kindergarten through Grade 12 are enrolled in the programme in the three provinces. Also as a result of Ukrainian community initiative, a Canadian Institute of Ukrainian Studies was established at the University of Alberta in 1976, proclaimed by its first director as "the cap on the Ukrainian educational ladder" and a bulwark against the "twin perils of Russification abroad and Anglo-Americanization at home." Since then, public funds have also gone toward a Chair of Ukrainian Studies at the University of Toronto and a Centre for Ukrainian Canadian Studies at the University of Manitoba. Ukrainians failed in their ultimate goal, however, to have minority language rights entrenched in the new Canadian constitution.

Multiculturalism grants to Ukrainian community organizations and the activities they sponsor have facilitated the expression of a Ukrainian element and identity in Canada. This is not to suggest that Ukrainian-Canadian ethnicity has either depended on public support in the past or is the product of the multiculturalism policies of the federal and provincial governments since the 1970s. From the days of first settlement, Ukrainians supported a myriad of community organizations and their activities, combining politics with culture, education and entertainment.

Nevertheless, recent years have seen many changes. Old-country politics failed to hold the Canadian born. Language loss deprived amateur theatricals and folk choirs

Ludmilla Temertey, 1944–
Ukrainian Welcome 1986

Lithograph
65.9 x 49.7 cm

Bread, salt and an embroidered ritual towel are important elements of a traditional Ukrainian welcome.

CCFCS 88-192

of both performers and audiences, Ukrainian churches of their congregations, and Ukrainian organizations of young members. Bingo was more entertaining than another lecture on one's national responsibilities, hockey practice more appealing than Saturday-morning Ukrainian school. At present, slightly less than one-half of Ukrainian Canadians belong to the Ukrainian (formerly Greek) Catholic and Orthodox churches and speak Ukrainian as their mother tongue; fewer speak Ukrainian as their home language; and in all three cases, they represent an aging group.

At the same time, non-verbal expressions of Ukrainianness are enjoying renewed life. Ukrainian folk dance has mushroomed in popularity, with schools in local communities across Canada teaching Ukrainian-Canadian youth dance steps from the Carpathian mountains and the Cossack steppes. Sometimes, the stories they tell are from the Canadian Prairies, and often the dances are performed before appreciative non-Ukrainian audiences. Cooking and embroidery classes also testify to eager interest in things Ukrainian, and like dance, they draw non-Ukrainians as well as those who need to be taught in a formal setting what their ancestors learned as a matter of course. The mainstreaming of Ukrainian foods, dance and handicrafts is a measure of acceptance, of legitimization via the "Ukrainian" as opposed to the "Canadian" side of the hyphen.

'I'm quite a mix. Scottish and Lunenburg Deutsch on my father's side, Danish and Ukrainian on my mother's.'
'Unusual recipe.'
'Yeah. Ukrainian's the great spice.'

— W.O. Mitchell, *Ladybug, Ladybug...*, 1988

This sheepskin coat (*kozhukh*), made in Bukovyna, western Ukraine, circa 1890, is typical of the ones worn by many early Ukrainian pioneers in western Canada.

88 cm H

CCFCS 71-156

A parade float, east-central Alberta, circa 1920.

Courtesy Ukrainian Cultural and Educational Centre, Winnipeg, Manitoba (Ivan Bobers'kyj Archive Collection)

Research suggests that a cultural ethnic consciousness and not a politicized national consciousness best defines contemporary Ukrainian-Canadian identity. Formal institutions and language, long declared by community spokespersons to be the key to meaningful group survival, have been found to be less important than selected primary synoptic symbols from the peasants' world. Enjoying the greatest staying power as best reflecting the unique shared experience of the group and most successfully bridging past and present are things like food, embroidery and Easter eggs — things visible and tangible. Food, so closely identified with the family while uniting its members in a larger communion, forms a particularly significant bond and aspect of Ukrainianness. Politically inoffensive, such symbols are compatible with what is apparently a satisfactory grassroots definition of multiculturalism as a showcase of Canadians' cultural heritages.

Ukrainian Canadians of today are unrecognizable as descendants of turn-of-the-century peasant immigrants. They are more apt to be urban than rural, to wear blue jeans than sheepskin coats and to listen to pop music and drink Coca Cola than to relate to or recognize the culture of a distant and unvisited homeland. As they celebrate their centenary, Ukrainian Canadians can look back proudly on their contributions to Canada and be assured that they are leaving a rich and distinct heritage for future generations.

DINNER
$5.00

Wsevolod W. Isajiw

ETHNIC ART AND THE UKRAINIAN-CANADIAN EXPERIENCE

Ethnic art records and interprets human experience. Several kinds of art fall into this category: folk art, naive art, professional art and souvenir art.

Folk art reflects a community's reaction to the world around it—to nature, the human life cycle and the routines of everyday life. It encodes in carvings, embroidery, drawings, dancing, singing and storytelling a community's conception of the world and serves to validate and teach about its experiences and its struggles with the basic questions of life. Folk art is thus inherently connected with religious beliefs and rituals.

A good example of Ukrainian folk art is the Easter egg. Traditionally such eggs depict stars and particularly the "high star"—the sun—a source of light and life and perhaps the most popular symbol in Ukrainian folk art. Long lines, which may be composed of repeated symbols (a long line of crosses, for instance) represent long life or eternity; and light or dark colours may refer to the bright or dark moments of life. These may be visual statements of well-wishing or of warning. After the introduction of Christianity, crosses, pictures of churches and religious inscriptions began to appear as motifs on the eggs. Byzantine-style Christian iconography was readily accepted in Ukraine because its symbolic style was similar to that of the folk art of the people. The decorated Easter egg, like a religious icon, has meaning beyond its form and invites the viewer to decode its message.

(opposite page)

Natalka Husar, 1951–
Heritage Display 1985

Acrylic on canvas
191 x 124 cm

CCFCS 87-71

Why does folk art persist in Canada, within an ethnic group that has long left its place of origin, that is surrounded by other cultures and whose members by now are

(left)

Molly Lenhardt, 1920–
Our Heritage 1980

Acrylic on wood
52.6 x 42.9 x 2.1 cm

CCFCS 80-208

(right)

Ann Harbuz, 1908–1989
Ten Weddings circa 1984

Oil on canvas
104.0 x 70.7 x 2.3 cm

CCFCS 84-377

predominantly urban dwellers? The answer is that folk art continues to perform several important functions for the Ukrainian community.

Folk art invites the viewer to affirm the meaning of life. Symbols suggesting circular motion, such as the star or the circle, are fundamental in Ukrainian folk art and refer to the life cycle of human existence—the cycle of seasons, of days followed by nights, sunshine followed by rain, birth, growth and maturity followed by death and so on. All these appear in some kind of repetitive continuity. Indeed, repetition can be considered a universal symbol of life itself and underlies the idea of rhythm. Thus folk art is a way of creating and re-creating the experience and emotion of a collective celebration of life.

The decoration of functional objects is a common practice in folk art. The instruments that make life possible are thus linked with the rituals that highlight the life cycle. The tool can acquire meaning that transcends its specific, narrow function, and a social occasion, a higher, religious value. In this way everyday ordinary activities take on a special, universal significance.

Folk art has another important function that contributes to its survival. When placed in a situation in which a distinct community wishes to revive its ethnic sentiments and traditions, for example on occasions celebrating heritage, folk art emerges as an important expression of this ethnicity.

The dividing line between folk art and naive art is not always clear. **Naive art** usually focuses on the community rather than the world around it, often in order to acknowledge and celebrate the community experience. For example, Molly Lenhardt's *Our Heritage* presents a "Ukrainian beauty" to be admired, and uses symbols dear to Ukrainians —the Ukrainian blue and yellow flag, sheaves of wheat, a cherry orchard, embroidered blouse and apron—to acknowledge the community as whole. Other works portray the community with emphatic exaggeration. For example, Ann Harbuz's *Ten Weddings* portrays ten wedding parties amidst a mixture of old and new—pioneer dwellings and a village are juxtaposed with modern high-rises, a horse-drawn plough contrasts with automobiles, and more. The community comes to be celebrated, as it were, ten times over.

The feature that distinguishes **professional art** from other forms of ethnic art is its ability to raise questions, to comment and sometimes to suggest alternative ways of thinking. Professional art may deal with nature, with people or with the artist's self. The visual presentation can entail contrasts, juxtapositions or abstractions. A nostalgic work about nature, a contrast between the natural and the human-made, and the reduction of reality to lines and rectangles are all possible treatments in this art form. A recurring theme in professional art is the problems of the ethnic experience.

Pavlo Lopata, 1945–
Ukrainian Golgotha 1982

Oil tempera
64.4 x 64.3 cm

CCFCS 88-180

Paul Demeda, 1960–
Girl with Sunglasses circa 1982

Lithograph
50.9 x 40.6 cm

CCFCS 88-165

Shawna Balas, 1961–
Before the Concert 1984

Watercolour
76.3 x 58.5 cm

CCFCS 88-125

Jeanette Shewchuk's *It Was a Long Time, It Was a Hard Time* captures the pain of immigration, showing an anxious family holding on to its few, precious possessions, facing an unknown future. A work may also comment on painful or unjust experiences in a highly symbolic fashion. Pavlo Lopata's *Ukrainian Golgotha* presents the history of Ukraine as a bard's lament; it shows the bard playing a *bandura* before an audience of young and old. The song becomes a historical epic that alludes to the crucifixion of Christ, who holds the destiny of Ukraine in his hands.

The ethnic experience often involves the tension of integration, accommodation and assimilation. A variety of

Sophia Lada, 1941–
Mavka [Woodland Nymph] 1989

Gouache
35.5 x 30.5 cm
Gift of Dr. Matthew and Anna Huta, Toronto

CCFCS 90-21

possible conflicts fosters a context within which professional art tends to view the contemporary as being incongruous with the traditional. For example, John Paskievich in his *Beer Bottle Cupola* angrily decries hedonistic substitutes for spiritual values. Elizabeth Jaworski in *Flowered Trio* uses the folk symbol of the wreath, which symbolizes beauty and "crowning glory," and places it on the heads of geese; a goose, however, in folk wisdom represents pretension without much substance. Thus the artist may be wondering how much real ethnic identity lies beneath the external decorative paraphernalia.

John Paskievich, 1947–
Beer Bottle Cupola 1988

Photograph
35.1 x 27.6 cm

CCFCS 88-179

The possibility of a conflict between one's ethnic identity and modern, technological daily life is pointedly raised and commented upon by both Shawna Balas' *Before the Concert* and Paul Demeda's *Girl with Sunglasses.* Is one's ethnic identity just a show, or is it real? Like a folk costume can it be put on for special occasions and taken off for "real" life?

Sophia Lada tries to resolve the problem of ethnic identity by delving into the remote the past. She explores the mythology of Ukraine's prehistoric ancestors to whom the spirits of nature gave wisdom and direction. Similarly, other artists search for historical symbols of identity, in Canada's pioneer Ukrainian heritage.

Natalka Husar is less mystical in her treatment of Ukrainian-Canadian heritage. *Heritage Display* shows a common type of collective ethnic expression, the ethnic festival. Two aging ladies sell tickets at an ethnic dinner; they are the typical guardians of the community's ethnic identity. But they are oblivious to a costumed figure hanging upside-down beside them. Husar objectifies her ethnic identity along with its inherent conflicts and turmoil. A similar trend can be seen in Ben Wasylyshen's *Prairie Madonna—Ternopil.* In this work ethnic identity is again represented by a woman dressed in a traditional costume; suspended in the air, legless, she gazes at a fading pioneer past symbolized by a cabin on the horizon.

The romanticization and commemoration of the pioneer experience are often themes in ethnic art. Lillian Parobec-Dzwonyk's *Homestead Icehouse*, for example, conveys a sense of nostalgia through the use of various images: the pioneer cabin, the winter setting to portray the harshness of survival, the embroidery to show ethnic roots, and the oil lamp to symbolize pioneer life and the ancestors' wisdom.

Although highly subjective and individualistic, professional ethnic art offers many original insights into the ethnic experience. These personal perspectives are often accepted as valid by the community and become part of a universal perception of the group and the culture.

Souvenir art, sometimes referred to as applied or commercial art, or simply kitsch, is usually inexpensive and produced for mass consumption. It often imitates folk, naive or professional art, making these other forms of ethnic art available to the people. Some examples are objects like mugs, plates, tablecloths, and spoons incorporating ethnic art motifs.

(left)

Ben Wasylyshen, 1961–
Prairie Madonna — Ternopil 1989

Serigraph
50.7 x 38.1 cm
Gift of the artist

CCFCS 89-385

(below)

Elizabeth Jaworski, 1937–
Flowered Trio circa 1987

Watercolour
71.5 x 57.2 cm

CCFCS 88-176

Nick Nykilchuk, 1931–
To Your Health circa 1984

Lithograph
35.4 x 27.7 cm
Gift of the artist

CCFCS 88-184

Souvenir art is also an inexpensive way of representing the community's ethnic identity to the wider society. It provides a visitor with a token that symbolizes the community and its culture. The viewers may belittle these souvenirs as bad art; however, those of Ukrainian background will probably admit to feeling tugs at their Ukrainian heart strings when gazing on some of these works. For example, Nick Nykilchuk's *To Your Health* shows frolicsome grandparents as caricatures and may invite the contradictory reactions, laughter and reverence.

Ethnic art comprises diverse forms of artistic expression. It is characterized by its focus on ethnic experience, a multifaceted phenomenon. Some forms express certain aspects of this experience better than others. Viewers may not equally appreciate all forms of ethnic art. Nonetheless a deepened appreciation of ethnic art can serve to promote a better understanding of ethnicity and of art in general.

Voyage

Locked in my berth as though it were
my coffin. I retched emptiness
itself. The other women took turns
helping the sick, keeping the children clean.

My daughters ran free over the ship
making friends with the sailors, who remembered
their own children, and were kind. 'Mother, get up,
come up to the deck; in the wind you'll feel better.
There's dancing, the sailors play accordion.'
I shut my eyes and prayed to die.

By the time the boat came into the harbour
I was able to wash and dress myself, hold down
a little bread. Before we could leave there had to be
inspection. Department of Immigration, Department
of Infectious Diseases. Loud, purple stamps.

They didn't explain, just motioned us
into separate rooms, men and women.
Strip to skin—babies, even the very old.
I had never been naked to any eyes
but the night's. We stumbled, walking past the doctors,
turning our eyes away. But I saw the old women,
breasts, bellies like emptied sacks:
skin aprons tied around their bones.

In the train from Halifax to Toronto
we sit up through a day and a night. The countryside spills
like rain off the windows. One strangeness
after another. Land without hedges or fences,
trees that have no names.

Coats buttoned to the chin, hands gloved,
our hats pulled down. We have shown
enough of ourselves to strangers.

— Janice Kulyk Keefer, *Fields*, 1989
In memory of Olena Levkovich and Tomasz Solowski

Jeanette Shewchuk, 1948–
It Was a Long Time, It Was a Hard Time circa 1987

Oil on canvas
51.0 x 40.8 cm

CCFCS 87-88

ΜΡ
ΘΥ

Dmytro V. Stepovyk

THE UKRAINIAN ICON IN CANADA

From the gallery I looked down on the scene before me. It was now broad daylight. The walls of the front of the church were covered with highly-colored ikons. Beneath the ikons, on shelf or pedestals, scores of tapers were burning. Near by were clustered the banners. Through the wide opening I saw into the alcove. On the fine linen of the altar were massive golden candlesticks, and books, and crucifixes. The priest in his gorgeous robes passed to and fro. The head-shawls of the women, as I looked down upon them, formed a moving mass of brilliant colors. The mingling of daylight and candle-light gave a touch of weirdness to the scene. It was a sight never to be forgotten.

— Miriam Elston, 1916
Methodist missionary worker among the Ukrainians
in east-central Alberta

If today one travels across the broad Canadian land from the Atlantic to the Pacific, visits large Ukrainian communities and farm families, stops at the numerous Ukrainian churches shining brightly on the horizon, a question soon emerges: How was it possible for poor emigrants from eastern Europe, having arrived at the end of the nineteenth century with only a few bundles of personal belongings, to have created in a hundred years such a dynamic and vital form of Christian art? It is equally astonishing that this small ethnic group was also able to preserve and foster its language, literature, music, folklore and fine arts.

(opposite page)

Protection of the Blessed Virgin Mary Ukrainian Greek Orthodox Church, near Wakaw, Saskatchewan, 1973.

CMC 74-16984

(inset)

Taras G. Snihurowycz, 1918–
Our Lady of the Sign 1989

Acrylic on copper sheet
51.5 x 43.0 cm

This icon shows Mary, the Mother of God, with the child Jesus.

CCFCS 89-32

Holy Ascension Orthodox Church, near Sturgis, Saskatchewan, 1972. Early Ukrainian pioneers attended services in simple log churches such as this one built in 1905.

CMC 74-16561

The ability of the Ukrainian immigrants to survive in the new land did not come about by renouncing their identity. Indeed, they brought with them and maintained ancient traditions, a unifying spiritual ideal and a highly developed cultural structure, which stood them in good stead. However, the Ukrainians not only preserved their culture, but enriched and developed it as well. They were generally open, cooperative and willing to learn from others.

The first Ukrainian immigrants to Canada were peasants from such regions of Ukraine as Bukovyna, Transcarpathia, Galicia and Volyn. Their native folk culture was manifested in handicrafts, native art, and oral and written folklore. In Canada, they built churches and painted icons and wall murals in the traditional spirit of their native land. With no professional architects or artists among them, it fell to the more creative with excellent memories of their traditional culture to be the local masters. Even so, the Ukrainian icon in Canada developed as a natural continuation of the thousand-year history of icon painting in Ukraine.

The early iconostases (decorative partitions) were as simple as the churches that housed them. Few of these churches, which once dotted the landscape of central and western Canada still exist. Individual icons and fragments of “royal doors” from these iconostases can be found. The surviving icons are typical of traditional icon painting in nineteenth-century Ukraine; stylistically they are a folkloric

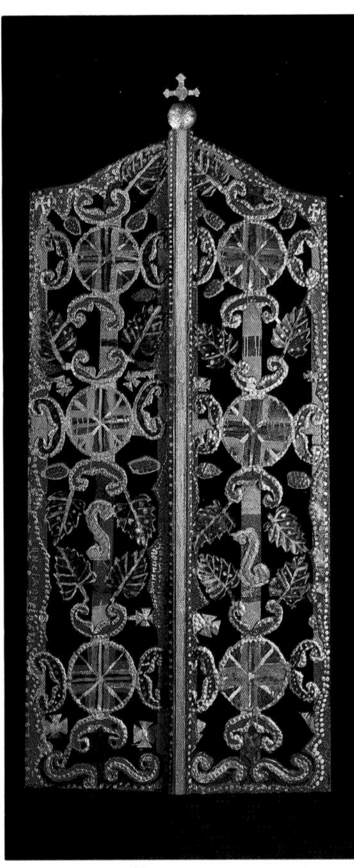

interpretation of the classical style of a professional artist. The "Slavic-Europeanized" features of Jesus Christ, the Holy Mother of God and the saints, the three-dimensional portrayal of figures, and the oil-on-canvas or wood medium all testify to an adherence of the early Ukrainian-Canadian icon painters to the traditions of their homeland. These icons also display traditional styles and motifs specific to the various regions of Ukraine from whence these immigrant artists came.

In Ukraine, icon painting was controlled by the eparchial powers of the Church. Throughout Christianity, there were established canons of icon painting that governed this art, including strict adherence to firmly defined prototypes and prescribed ecclesiastical guidelines. Four artistic styles (Byzantine, Renaissance, baroque, classicism), used in different periods, governed iconography in Ukraine. In Canada no such guidelines for Ukrainian iconography existed. Here the early icon painters had to depend entirely on memory (unless a photograph of an iconographic work had been brought from Ukraine). The formalities of the art form and the historical significance and veneration of the icons were deeply ingrained in the people. These icons were not merely religious reminders of biblical events; they were imbued with spirituality transcending the material world and influenced greatly the faithful. As well, a true icon did not bear the name of the artist and these early Ukrainian-Canadian painters remain anonymous.

(left)

Iconostasis, made by Pavlo Zabolotnyi, circa 1930, Holy Trinity Ukrainian Orthodox Church, Canora, Saskatchewan, 1972.

CMC 74-16806

(right)

Royal Doors, 1911

Wood, metal, paint
202 x 93 cm
Gift of St. Elias the Prophet Ukrainian Greek Orthodox Church, Hamton, Saskatchewan

Opening to the sanctuary, royal doors represent the gateway to the kingdom of God.

CCFCS 72-189.1-2

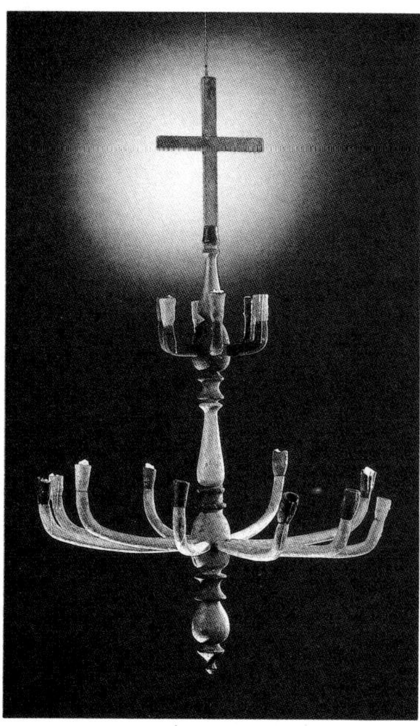

Chandelier, early 20th century, from a church in Saskatchewan. The Ukrainian word for chandelier is *pauk*, which means "spider."

Painted wood
100 x 55 x 55 cm
Gift of St. John the Baptist Ukrainian Greek Orthodox Church, Hamton, Saskatchewan

CCFCS 72-190

One of the first professional icon painters in Canada was Peter Lipinski (1888–1975). He came to Canada from Galicia, Ukraine, during the First World War. Lipinski had learned the skills and techniques of icon painting and ornamental decoration of church interiors in Ukraine. Throughout his long life, he decorated the interiors of over forty Ukrainian churches (iconostases, icons and wall murals) in Alberta, Saskatchewan and Manitoba. Lipinski's works reflect a classical style; he probably followed the icon-painting traditions of the Pochaiv Lavra, one of western Ukraine's oldest monasteries.

During his life Lipinski did not change his style of icon painting and continually perfected his mastery of the art. Although the first rural churches in Alberta for which he painted icons and wall murals no longer exist, some of his work is preserved in the Ukrainian Cultural Heritage Village Museum, near Edmonton, Alberta. These works show Lipinski's mastery of classical iconographic art. He strove to spiritual intensity in the facial features and liked to combine various shades of red and blue to create what he felt was a heightened religious feeling in his works.

During the 1920s Lipinski was perhaps the only professional Ukrainian icon painter in Canada. It is not known whether there were any students or followers of his art in Canada at that time. In the thirties, other artists began painting icons, among them Pavlo (Paul) Zabolotnyi and Stepan (Stephen) Meush. During this period Ukrainian-Canadian icon painters experimented freely in the area of stylistic synthesis, combining in their works any number of the four main styles that once flourished in Ukraine: Byzantine, Renaissance, baroque and classicism. An interesting array of icons, frescoes and mosaics, reflecting such style combinations as Byzantine-Renaissance, Renaissance-baroque and Byzantine-classicism, resulted. Classicism alone no longer served as the sole basis for icon painting.

After the Second World War, many Ukrainian churches were built in Canada to meet the spiritual needs of the new Ukrainian immigrants, and icon painting was revitalized. The reinterpretation, creative utilization and combination of the formal styles that had begun earlier intensified. At the same time, increased professionalism in icon painting brought with it a deeper appreciation and greater knowledge of the ancient Ukrainian icon. It became more apparent that there was a need to master the symbolism of the icon and the methods and styles of leading iconographers from various periods of Ukraine's history.

In recent years, artist-iconographers, in preparation for the celebration of the millennium of Ukrainian Christianity (A.D. 988–1988) increasingly drew their inspiration from icons, mosaics and frescoes of the tenth to the twelfth centuries and painted more often in the Byzantine style that dominated that period. Many new iconostases and wall murals in the Kievan Byzantine style were created in Canada. These works are distinguished by the original interpretation of this style and include other stylistic influences from later periods.

Processional Standard, 1915
Collected in Saskatchewan

Painted wood
185.4 x 59.7 cm

Ukrainian settlers used processional crosses, banners and standards as part of their church ritual. This standard features an angel's face surrounded by a halo from which wings extend; crossed wings appear above and below, for a total of six wings. The angel is perhaps a seraphim, a six-winged angel

CCFCS 67-37

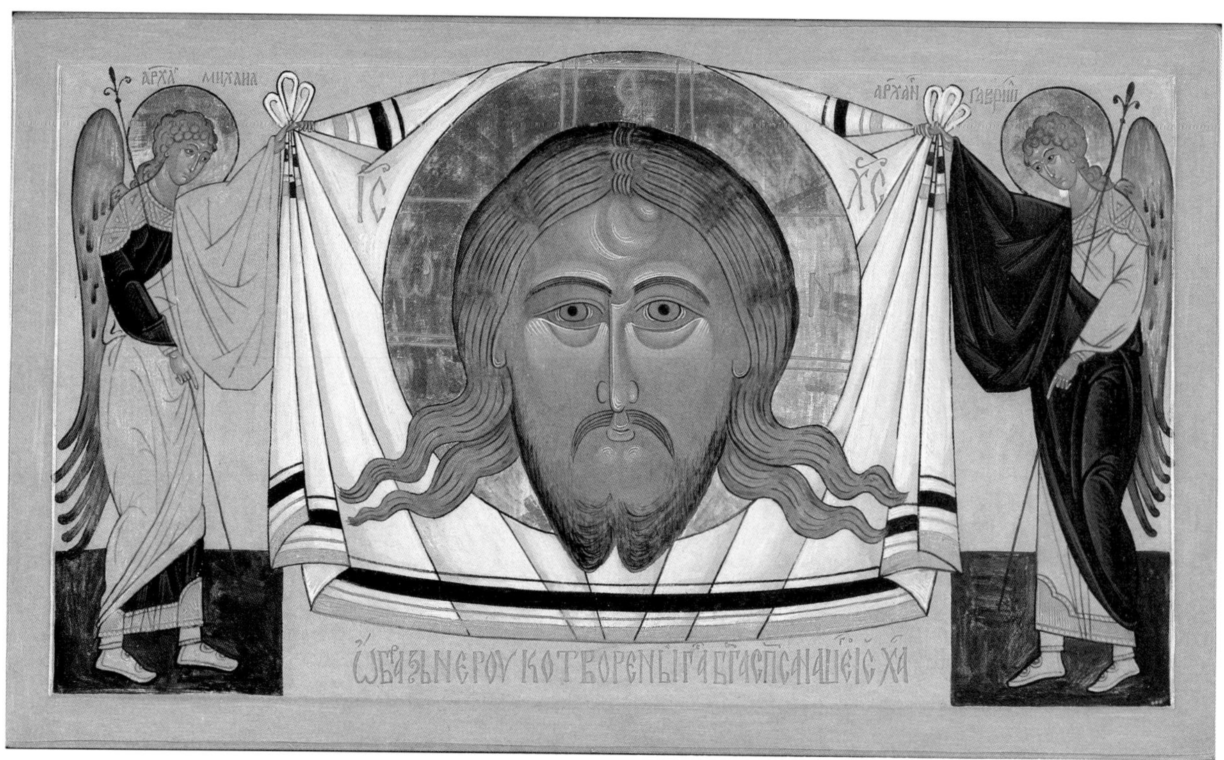

Heiko Schlieper, 1931–
The Vernicle 1981

Egg tempera and gold leaf on basswood
64.0 x 38.0 cm

According to legend, the image of Christ's face was impressed on a cloth given to him by St. Veronica on the way to his Crucifixion. In this icon, the archangels Michael and Gabriel hold this cloth, called the vernicle, or veronica. Below it is an inscription in Cyrillic meaning "Saviour not by hand created," which refers to the miraculous way the image was imprinted on the cloth.

CCFCS 88-173

Combining styles can often produce a confusing mixture of motifs. In Canada, however, this technique has been applied with much success. This is seen in the works of such early iconographic masters as Peter Lipinski, Tedor Baran, Yuluyan (Julian) Butsmanyuk and Vadym Dobrolizh, who successfully synthesized Renaissance, baroque and classical styles. The inclusion of the Byzantine style by later iconographers, such as Myron Levyts'kyi (Toronto), and Roman Kowal and Vera Senchuk (Winnipeg), was accomplished by developing original methods of complex stylization in frescoes, mosaics and icons. Their compositions are distinguished by lightness, upward Gothic inclinations and richness of colour.

Developed over several generations the Ukrainian icon in Canada is remarkable in its ability to be self-revitalized while maintaining its true spiritual nature. In the future, it may even inspire changes in church art in Ukraine as that country embarks on a new era.

Note: This article is a translation from Ukrainian.

Halyna Mordowanec-Regenbogen, 1945–
Icon of Jesus Christ 1975

Oil on canvas, glued on wood panel
38.2 x 26.6 cm
Gift of the Ukrainian Canadian Committee to Commemorate the Millennium of Christianity in Ukraine, Windsor, Ontario

Christ holds a book from the New Testament; to the left of his halo is the abbreviated word for "Jesus" in old Cyrillic and to the right the one for "Christ."

CCFCS 89-36

HAPPY EASTER
ХРИСТОС ВОСКРЕС
HARBUZ
1975

Michael Owen Jones

A Folklorist's Viewpoint on Ukrainian-Canadian Art

The mention of Ukrainian Easter eggs conjures up images of ritual objects created each spring, gaily coloured or ornamented with arcane symbols, and used ceremonially in church and at home. In Canada today, however, the Ukrainian Easter egg is produced at any time of the year, sawed in half or left whole and mounted in a picture frame, reproduced in paintings, or replicated as a massive object on a pedestal.

Similarly, wooden utensils, articles of old clothing and other objects are finding their way onto mantels and into display cases. Modern frames surround ancient icons, previously draped in traditional cloth. A plough that once broke sod on the western prairie becomes the subject of a painting and is shown as abandoned and rusting amidst a clump of weeds. A wagon wheel or milk can is now used to support a mailbox.

Is this the degeneration of a once vital heritage? Are these examples of distorted functions of objects whose original meanings have been lost or corrupted? When is an object "art"?

As epitomized by easel painting and gallery sculpture in the Euro-American elitist tradition, art supposedly elevates the mind, inspires the spirit and is to be appreciated for its formal perfection. (It must do these things, because lacking practicality and usefulness, it would have no purpose.) Framing transmutes an ordinary object into something "special." While protecting an object, a frame also acts as an interpretive device that creates and/or distorts meaning and significance by highlighting and preserving selected aspects of experience.

(opposite page)

Ann Harbuz, 1908–1989
Easter Egg 1976

Oil on Masonite
65.9 x 44.3 cm

CCFCS 80-421

Nicholas Bodnar, 1914–
The Walking Plough 1987

Oil on canvas
55.6 x 48.2 cm

CCFCS 89-39

The Euro-American art tradition constitutes far too narrow a basis on which to develop an understanding of universal creative processes and aesthetic responses. Perhaps the most far-reaching conception of art was set forth by Franz Boas based on his studies of Inuit and West Coast Indian traditions in Canada, research by one of his students, Ruth Bunzel, on Pueblo pottery in the United States, and investigations by their colleagues of traditional aesthetic forms elsewhere in the world. Boas and other researchers found little painting and sculpture in traditions outside Euro-American elitism and even less that was framed. He argued, however, that although objects like rawhide boxes, fur clothes and baskets were practical rather than contemplative in nature, these tools and products of tribal industry exhibited technical control over processes leading to excellence and formal perfection, just as easel paintings are presumed to do.

Following Boas we can define folk art as traditional behaviour that reveals an aesthetic impulse and a mastery of skills. Some forms and processes studied in recent years as folk art include creating and exchanging homemade cards

This framed egg clock was made by Ted and Eve Wasylyshen of Winnipeg, Manitoba, in 1988.

33 x 33 cm

CCFCS 88-128

This embroidery decorates the sleeve of a woman's blouse. Its geometric pattern is typical of the Hutsul region of western Ukraine.

Gift of the Ukrainian Heritage Association and Museum of Canada, Toronto

CCFCS 89-408.8

and gifts, canning and arranging jars of fruits and vegetables, painting scenes on window and door screens, serving ethnic or family dishes in the home, and carving pumpkins and making and displaying harvest figures at Halloween.

Another set of folk-art traditions consists of collecting and exhibiting souvenirs, memorabilia and benchmark objects. Bronzed baby shoes, birthday ribbons, graduation tassels, retirement plaques, post cards, and pictures in family photo albums or assembled as a collage and framed may possess great emotional significance and powers of evocation. Often encoding memories and messages, such objects and their aesthetic manipulation can contribute to the making, arranging and remaking of people's lives, identities, and sense of self.

Many people fondly preserve a tool, a kitchen utensil, a piece of furniture that ages with its owner, bric-a-brac, knick-knacks, and the odds and ends in china cabinets and on mantels. Valued more for what they signify than any intrinsic worth, they are collected and saved prospectively, with a sense of their future ability to recall memories.

Some individuals also create memory objects retrospectively. They bring together things with a personal history or a past personified, creating tableaux or assemblages as

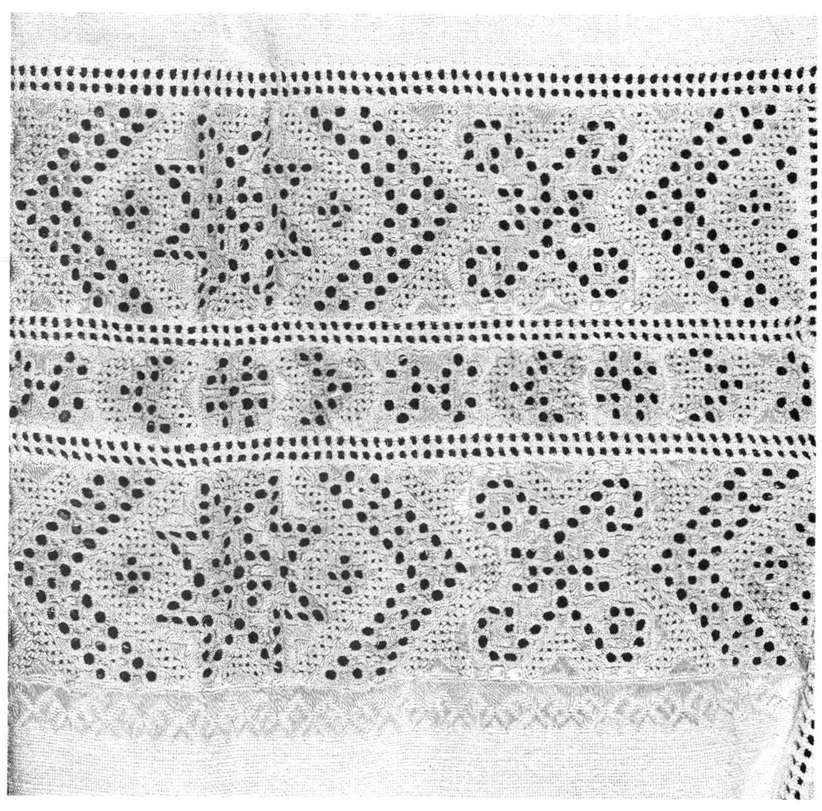

(left)

This embroidered floral design is from the sleeve of a woman's blouse and is typical of the Bukovynian region of western Ukraine.

CCFCS 82-440

(right, upper and lower)

Fancy cutwork on woman's blouse, with lower shot showing close-up of one of the designs.

Gift of the Ukrainian Heritage Association and Museum of Canada, Toronto

CCFCS 89-415.1

sculpted forms. Others draw or paint scenes from childhood, such as a farm, a market, annual holidays and life-cycle celebrations, thus making discrete moments of yesteryear a part of the present. Homes become living history museums; individuals, curators of their lives.

If souvenirs and memorabilia render the past authentic and serve as tools for remembering selective aspects of history, then collectables are authenticated by the past (although not necessarily by *their* past). No longer fashionable, usable or useful, these objects—these collectables—become collectable because of their relative scarcity nowadays and a mythification of their original purpose or value. Sometimes abandoned or discarded objects are used as raw material for new creations because of their particular meanings and associations.

Miniatures with their attention to detail excite the imagination for their virtuosity and may evoke myth-making, fantasies and role playing. Military figures, model trains and planes, and tiny cups and saucers, for example, inspire such behaviour. Often they are arranged into tableaux, heightening their evocative power.

Other ensembles are found stored away in drawers and boxes: collections of earrings, brooches, and necklaces, or business cards, theatre programmes, and movie tickets. Scraps of cloth that are stitched together are the quintessential example of assemblage as a synthetic memory object, and are known as quilts or "comforters."

These collections, ensembles and assemblages are tangible means by which experiences are extended through time, memories are preserved, or lives and relationships are held together, reflected on and perpetuated. They may provide a frame of reference and a sense of order, control and closure. Often they serve as "conversation pieces," a basis for interaction and communication.

These objects and activities are also traditional; that is, they are forms or processes that are repeated, reproduced or emulated and that evince continuities or consistencies in human thought and behaviour through time and space. All these actions or outcomes of behaviour are imbued with meaning. As examples of folklore and folk art they exhibit skill and a mastery of technique and are given aesthetic value.

The Ukrainian art tradition in Canada includes many examples of objects and displays that illustrate and exemplify these principles. One of the most significant forms of

... my major project — the history of Ukrainian settlement in Canada in a series of murals. This will be a labour of love for our people. Someone would have to donate one whole building for this purpose. And I would decorate the whole interior with murals something like... Sistine Chapel in Rome.

— William Kurelek, 1974

Ukrainian Easter eggs (*pysanky*) are known for their bold, vibrant colouring and intricate designs, ranging from repetitive geometric motifs to representational elements with religious, agrarian and mytho-zoomorphic connotations. Most of these are hens' eggs, dyed using the wax-resist method.

expression, not only of Ukrainian experience but also of Canadian identity, is the Easter egg and the complex of beliefs and customs in which it is embedded.

Although written sources do not document Easter eggs in what is now Ukraine until the thirteenth century (the

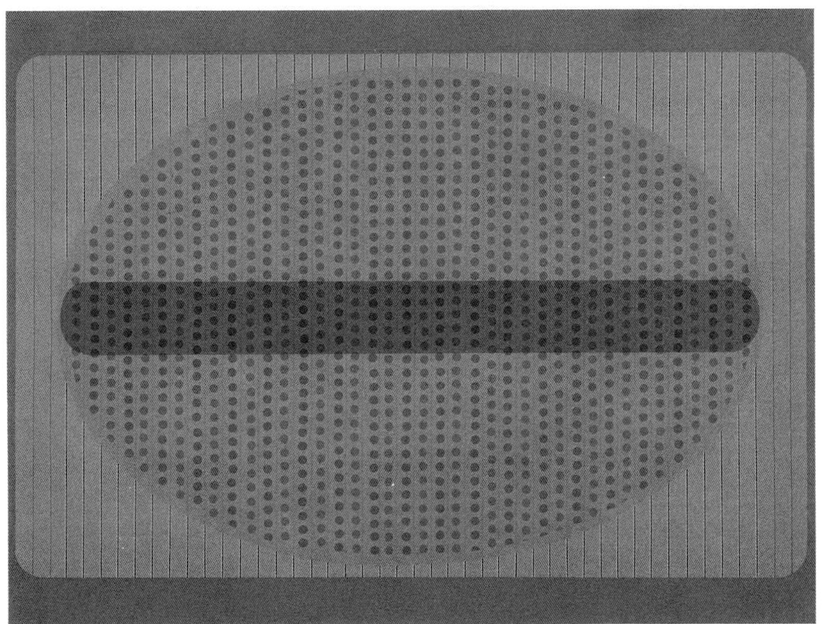

Tony Tascona, 1926–
Ukrainian Experience 1981

Serigraph
75.3 x 56.2 cm

CCFCS 88-172

Eastern Slavs were officially Christianized in A.D. 988), ancient burial mounds contain egg shells thought to have been placed there as magical talismans. Moreover, several designs on contemporary Ukrainian Easter eggs appear to be nearly identical to some motifs on pottery from Neolithic times.

The egg has long been an object of wonder and amazement, its smooth, symmetrical shell enclosing the mystery of newly forming life. The egg figures prominently in creation myths world wide. It symbolizes first consciousness, the creator gods and the universe arising from it.

In Ukrainian tradition two different kinds of eggs are generally prepared. The *krashanka* is an edible, hard-boiled egg dyed a single colour. The *pysanka*, on the other hand, is usually intended as ornamentation rather than food; the contents are left inside the egg or drained through a small hole.

Usually it is the simple, cooked *krashanka* that is eaten after a blessing ceremony at the local parish church. The oldest member of the family initiates the Easter feast by cutting up the blessed Easter egg into as many portions as there are household members. The *pysanky* are typically given as gifts or tokens of appreciation and friendship, or kept for decorative purposes in the household.

... at length in the bosom abysmal
Of Darkness an egg, from whirlwind conceived,
Was laid by the sable plumed Night.
And out of that egg, as the seasons evolved,
Sprang love...

—Aristophanes, 414 B.C.

Common designs on *pysanky* include celestial bodies, plants and vegetation, animals and humans or their features, religious symbols, and tools or implements. In 1967, centennial Ukrainian Easter eggs commemorating one hundred years of Canadian Confederation were produced in western Canada. Today some eggs are inscribed with the Lord's Prayer. An archaic style of ornamentation characterized by coarse lines, imperfect coloration and agricultural motifs has given way to a greatly refined version with richer colouring, precision of line and detailed symmetry. New ceremonial and ritual uses have developed. Ukrainian ornamented eggs may be seen at church sales, at folk festivals or during the Yuletide season, when they are given as Christmas gifts. Some eggs are wooden, thus eliminating the problem of breakage. Others are sequestered away, put on display in large goblets or set in plush-lined cases.

Reportedly, each village and family in Ukraine had its own particular designs and techniques, transmitted through the generations and executed in secret away from the eyes of inquisitive neighbours. In this respect, there is no single design or motif that everyone in Ukraine learned and executed. A similar situation exists in Canada, since those of Ukrainian descent here derive from various communities and regions of Ukraine and represent the entire range of immigrant identity from foreign born to second or third (or more) generation; moreover, many non-Ukrainians make Ukrainian Easter eggs.

Nevertheless, a Ukrainian Easter egg that is the quintessential of Ukrainian values, accomplishments and identity is popularly thought to exist. How this assumption originated and developed into an ideal of ethnic purity needs further research. A possible contributing factor is that Ukrainians in Canada have been sufficiently numerous to maintain many of their old-country traditions. Easter holidays, celebrated by the majority of Canadians, were easy to continue. The egg is widely recognized as a symbol of rebirth, so it persists in annual spring rites as an object of veneration regardless of one's ethnicity. Coloured, hard-boiled Easter eggs usually are eaten; ornamented, uncooked ones tend to break; there is thus a recurrent need to replenish the supply of eggs at Easter, helping assure the continuation of the tradition. Moreover, the "tradition" comprises a supporting complex not just of objects but also of customs, beliefs, and rituals; it is participated in by people of all ages and involves a range of emotions from great solemnity to unrestrained joyousness.

The Ukrainian Easter egg syndrome in Canada may have produced side effects considered by some as undesirable. Because of the widely acclaimed artistry of *pysanky*, Ukrainians have been typecast in the role of *pysanka* makers, with little attention to their other art forms and little regard for the Easter egg traditions of other ethnic groups.

Cultural representation is an important issue for many people. Stereotypes develop easily, presenting members of a particular group as one-dimensional. On the other hand, the process of cultural identification through the manipulation of selected symbols may result in considerable ingenuity in the service of aesthetics, increased visibility or self-promotion (whether of a person, community or organization).

Ukrainian identity and Canadian identity are sometimes juxtaposed in Easter egg art. One example is an art composition consisting of a maple leaf and an ornamented

The two identities side by side, created in 1988 by Ted and Eve Wasylyshen of Winnipeg, Manitoba.

18.3 x 18.3 x 3.5 cm

CCFCS 88-126

Chester Kuc, 1931–
Halya and Ivanko 1986

Embroidered silk-mesh
35 x 24 cm

This miniature version of a Ukrainian ritual towel is intended for decorative purposes. The verse in Ukrainian Cyrillic tells of the maiden Halya being courted by the enamoured Ivanko.

CCFCS 88-161

Easter egg (sawed in half), matted and framed. Another is the "world's largest *pysanka,*" located at Vegreville, Alberta, and erected in honour of the Royal Canadian Mounted Police's hundredth anniversary (1874–1974). Nearly 9 metres long and more than 5.5 metres wide, it weighs 2270 kilograms. Reads one postcard: "It spectacularly contrives to combine the ancient traditions of one of Alberta's largest ethnic groups with architectural and geometric developments that represent 'break-throughs' in modern science, thus linking heritage and progress."

Cynics might contend that much of this artistic activity is gratuitous and without any clear social use. They might insist that painted images of ploughs or *pysanky*, decorated Easter eggs on postcards or posters, or other examples of "framed heritage" convert important experiences into mere souvenirs, memorializing an imperiled continuity that these phenomena too are responsible for disrupting. They might lament the apparent reduction of a great tradition to sentimental and talismanic uses in pathetic attempts to promote nostalgia, or worse, as not taking an ethnic identity and cultural heritage seriously.

In the final analysis, expressions of Ukrainian identity and culture in Canada have been affected by many processes and experiences. The waves of immigration were composed of individuals from different families, villages and regions in Ukraine; and they occurred at different periods that saw changes in the Old World as well as the New. Emigrants from rural areas in the nineteenth century and those who fled towns and cities in the middle of the twentieth century had to have had different experiences, values and traditions. Not surprisingly, therefore, "Ukrainian-Canadian" culture is and always was a multifaceted, layered phenomenon.

Formal education and cultural institutions have, of course, affected people's perceptions of what "art" is; but there is also the common human experience of seeing something framed by tree limbs or rock formations, and the natural inclination when giving aesthetic value to human activities to appreciate a thing for its form alone, for associations with it, or both. Popular culture and the mass media often "mediate" a tradition, taking it from people's everyday lives, altering it in accord with other values and purposes, and turning it around for consumption. If the print and electronic media have ignored the single-coloured *krashanka* as well as the customs involved in Easter, they have stimulated the artistic refinement of the *pysanka*, thereby elevating the decorated Easter egg to a level of achievement of which anyone identifying with a Ukrainian heritage may be proud. And, as always, in this public acclaim lies the celebration of not just one group but of the whole human race.

Zenon S. Pohorecky

Reflections on the Folkways of Canada's Early Ukrainian Settlers

Today's middle-class mythology often recalls Ukrainian immigrant dreams of a land of promise and stereotypes early Ukrainian pioneers on the Prairies as illiterate peasants, too poor to have much more than the old-fashioned clothes they wore and a few things locked in trunks, bric-a-brac like homemade jewelry or beeswax candles. That these early immigrants were materially poor is for the most part true. But each one of them also brought a vast inner world of know-how, folklore and wisdom.

Except for the harsher winters and drier summers, the Canadian Prairies are in many ways like the forest-steppe region of Ukraine. The landscape would have seemed familiar to those first Ukrainian immigrants. They could even find some of the same medicinal herbs and plants. Old-country folkways were retained in the new land and made survival and settlement easier.

For spiritual survival in Canada, the first Ukrainian settlers brought crosses and icons draped with embroidered towels. Such portable icons could be placed in a sacred corner of the home. Their priests, however, remained in Ukraine. Without priests, why build churches?

Some of the older community members recall a period in Canada when there were no roads, no basic necessities and, more importantly, no churches. Canada's first Ukrainians filled their winter loneliness with prayers chanted inside their dugout homes. In summer, some gathered in forest meadows on important religious occasions; many such sites are now commemorated with crosses, shrines or churches. They also assembled at cemeteries for funerals and spring

(opposite page)

A typical Bukovynian family dressed in festive costume, Wasel, Alberta, circa 1920.

Orshinsky Collection

(left)

A grave marker with an inscription in Cyrillic, circa 1929, from a Ukrainian cemetery in Saskatchewan.

Cast concrete
118.2 x 56.4 x 13.7 cm

CCFCS 83-1768

(right)

Cemetery at Ukrainian Greek Orthodox Church of the Assumption of the Blessed Virgin Mary, near Stenen, Saskatchewan, 1972.

CMC 74-16750

rites (*zeleni svjata*). Cemeteries came first. The need for a burial place for the dead took precedence over building a church for the living.

An early prairie church while being suitable as a House of God also had to be practical and affordable. The cost of building and furnishing even a modest church was high, given the meagre resources of these pioneers. Some community members pledged part of their income, mortgaged their homes, gave land or helped by signing loans and credit notes for building materials. The first churches were made of logs and clay, with the men, women and children of the community contributing their untutored skills as labourers, carpenters and artisans to re-establish their village church.

The inside of most of the early wooden churches in Canada were decorated according to traditional iconography. However, few parishes could afford to hire a professional artist for this purpose. Usually, churches were decorated over several years in a piecemeal fashion, sometimes by different artists, creating a distinctive look for each church. The embroidering of altar cloths, church banners, and towels (*rushnyky*) for adorning icons was a task traditionally done by women.

Church artist Jacob Maydanyk (1891–1984) is perhaps better known for the cartoon character Vujko Shtif (Uncle Steve), which he created in 1915. For decades he painted icons, many of them in a sunny studio atop his Providence Church Goods shop by the noisy CPR subway on North Main

Street in Winnipeg. As he painted icons, he regaled visitors with tall tales over shots of rye; his Christ would sometimes look like a cossack and his Virgin Mary like the hapless heroine, Kateryna, from an epic poem by the national poet of Ukraine, Taras Shevchenko. Some of his motifs hid nationalist symbols, such as tridents disguised as leaves.

The early immigrants dressed as they would have in Ukraine—in an ancient peasant style that adapted local materials to suit the season. Light summer garb was made of cool linen from woven flax, while winter wear was of sheep's wool, leather and fur. The men wore straw hats in summer and brimless felt or fur hats in winter. A woman's head covering depended on her marital status: an unmarried woman had braided or loose hair, held with a band of wool or linen decorated with a wreath of flowers on festive occasions; a married woman always covered her head with a kerchief or scarf.

Garments were white or grey with bright embroidered collars and sleeves. The shirt was a simple design, having a

Liz Bykowski, 1941–
Friends, 1987

Acrylic on canvas, glued on Masonite
78.3 x 57.7 cm
Gift of the artist

CCFCS 89-45

rectangular body, and sleeves fitted to shoulder pieces and gussets. The embroidery imitated the rich brocades of old-country nobles; decorative stitches kept seams in place. The woman's sleeve embroidery was especially ornate and her shirt reached mid-calf.

In Canada the wearer of this brightly decorated clothing was easily recognized as a member of the Ukrainian community and often became the target of ethnic slurs and discrimination. Soon traditional garb was replaced by cheap factory-made calico. Old-country clothing was closeted in community halls across Canada, reappearing from time to time on the immigrant stage.

Nowadays, Ukrainian costumes are specially designed for stage performances and donned by thousands of folk dancers. Men's embroidered shirts are worn as symbols of ethnicity and are sometimes presented as gifts to dignitaries. Ironically, the embroidered shirt of the peasant immigrant has become an expensive and stylish item of clothing, and the

Complete with musicians, ritual towel and bread, a welcome party awaits the bridal couple, near Ethelbert, Manitoba, circa 1951.

CMC 85-3629

sheepskin coat, which once kept the poor immigrant settler warm, appears as an ethnic symbol in works of art displayed with pride in the living rooms of middle-class suburbia.

Food is an important part of many Ukrainian celebrations and rituals. Easter Sunday baskets overflow with batiked eggs (*pysanky*), and foods on embroidered towels are blessed at dawn in churchyards. *Pasky* (Easter loaves) and *babky* (sweetened breads) are baked especially for this day. In ancient times, such activities celebrated the return of spring; now they symbolize the Resurrection. Similarly the twelve meatless dishes in a Christmas Eve supper that recall the twelve apostles probably have their origins in earlier times. One of these Christmas dishes is *kutya*, a gruel made of wheat, honey and poppy seed; the father throws a spoonful of the gruel at the ceiling in the hope that it will stick — a sign of good luck in the year ahead.

The Ukrainian immigrants supplemented their traditional foods with tasty fare from nature. Children gathered the broad leaves of dandelions and other common plants for mother to serve raw, to make *holubtsi* (leaf rolls with grain fillings) or to cook into an appetizing "spinach.". After a summer shower, they searched for mushrooms — the *kozari*

William Kurelek, 1927–1977
Field sketch of pioneer church, Chipman, Alberta, 1973.

Charcoal on paper
49.5 x 39.4 cm

CCFCS 74-771

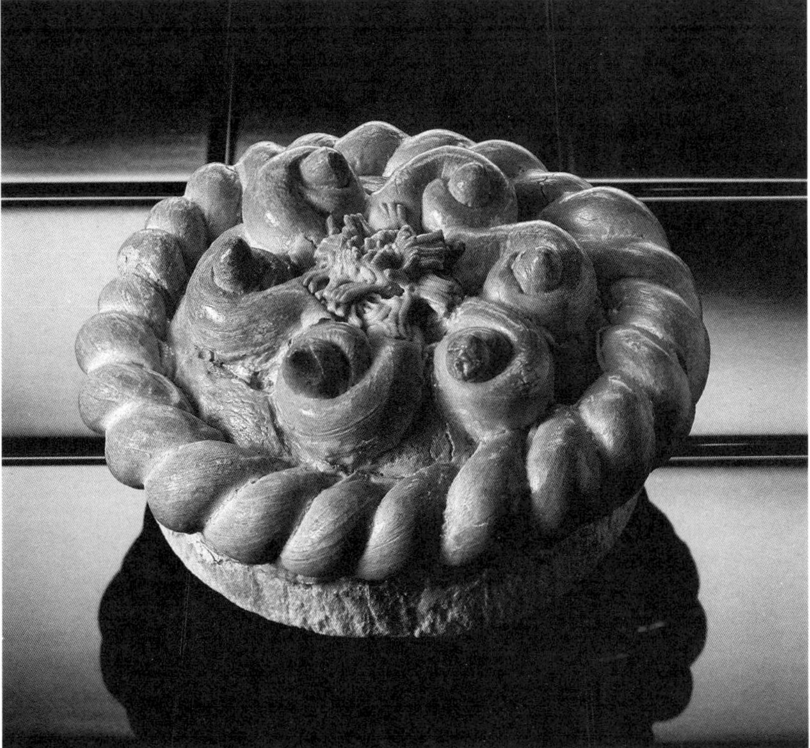

Decorated breads, like this Easter *paska*, are part of many Ukrainian ceremonies and rituals.

18 (diam.) x 6 cm
Gift of Ann Harbuz, North Battleford, Saskatchewan

CCFCS 84-242

in Saskatchewan's aspen groves or the *pidpen'ky* among Manitoba's oaks. Children learned by watching their parents discard the toxic ones and thus the tradition was passed on. In 1898 a government agent reportedly saw newly arrived Ukrainians "gather toadstools and fungus in the woods." They still do.

Some of the foods the Ukrainian immigrants ate were seen by the wider society as peculiar or even contemptible. For example, they were vilified for spicing their food with garlic. At one time, it is rumoured, its scent was considered so intolerable that there was a move to ban it from Winnipeg streetcars. The potent Ukrainian homebrew, *samohonka,* was declared illegal by Canadian officials, although it had been traditionally distilled for rituals associated with weddings, funerals and hospitality. Only *varenyky* or *pyrohy* (boiled or pan-fried dumplings) and borscht (a beet-based soup) could be served without fear, or so it seemed.

The Ukrainians preserved food in several ways. They dried peas, grapes, figs, plums, mushrooms, meats, sunflower and pumpkin seeds; pickled eggs, meats, beets, cabbage,

This plane (*hembil'*), with carved ornamentation, was made and used by a pioneer Ukrainian settler in Manitoba, early 20th century.

Wood, metal
32.5 x 6.0 x 6.0 cm

CCFCS 71-716

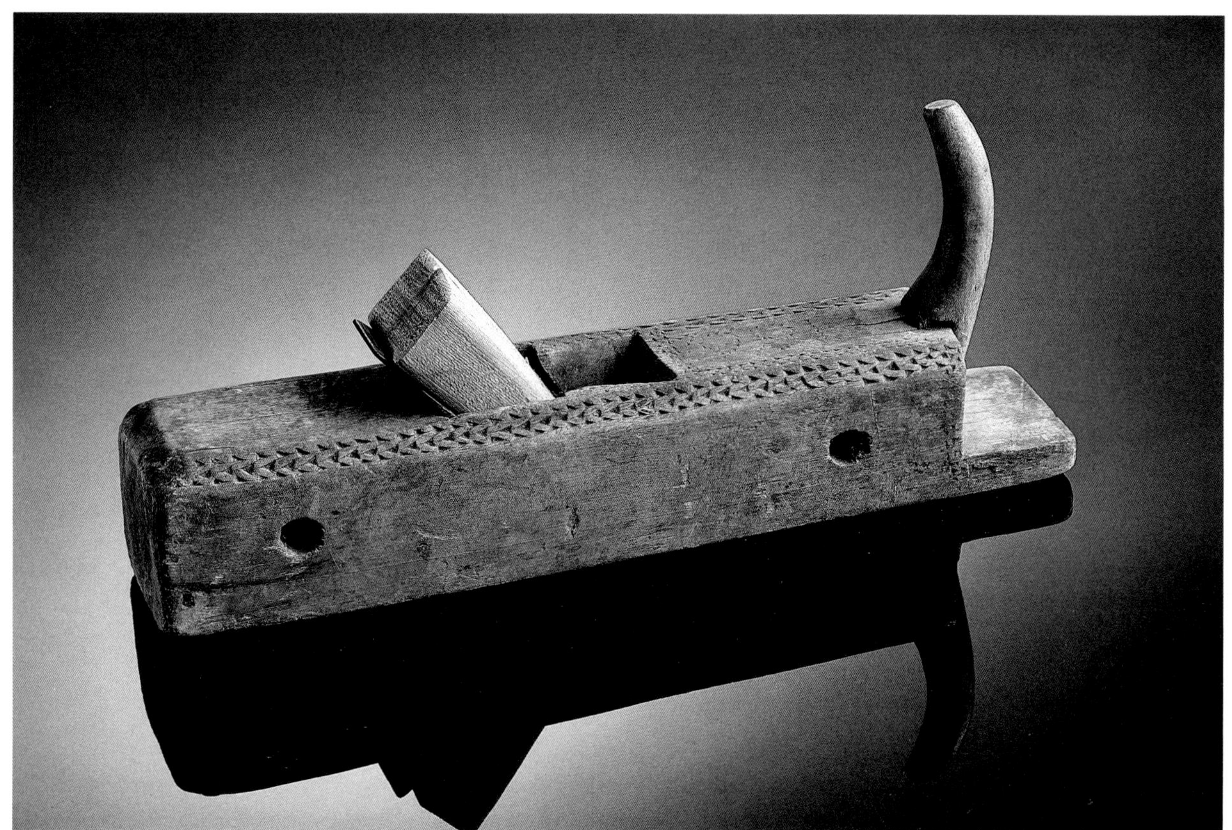

cucumbers or mushrooms; canned fruit or cabbage in jars; and stored foods in barrels (for example, borscht), in smokehouse attics (sausages) or in root cellars (for example, potatoes).

Swine, sheep, goats, chickens, ducks and geese were raised, generating such products as eggs, fowl, pork, ham and bacon. Cows were more valued for milk than for meat. In Ukraine, wild animals were rarely eaten, but in the new country, the poor settler could not be so choosy. Moose, deer and other animals were hunted and the meat shared by the community. Carp was abundant in prairie rivers and the Ukrainians also enjoyed the whitefish, grayling, trout, sturgeon and pike they found here. All such wild foods added much-needed protein to the diet of the immigrants.

Traditional dishes were generally inexpensive but took time to make. Recipes were transmitted orally from generation to generation. Today Ukrainian Canadians usually prepare traditional dishes only for special events and from recipe books. Ukrainian food is now part of Canada's culinary heritage.

Many of the early Ukrainian immigrants in Canada lived in dugouts. Such a *buda* or *burdej* was used centuries ago by lone cossacks monitoring Mongol incursions. Hermits and paupers also lived in such pit-huts until the nineteenth century. In Canada, such a hut sometimes housed seventeen. In Ukraine, multiple units, linked by doors, had evolved over many centuries into thatch dwellings with plank floors and log walls plastered with clay and limed in spring. A family-room's clay oven (*pich*) occupied an entire wall and included a baking oven, a metal cooking plate, and a flat top, used to bed children because its thick wall retained heat after the fire had died out.

People from the same village or district in Ukraine tended to live close together on the Prairies. They formed work bees to build their houses, which could take two men up to three months to complete. The plastering of the log exterior was done by women and could be completed in just a few days.

A traditional house was energy and cost efficient. It needed minimal capital to build, most labour and building materials being available at no cost: timber, clay, sand, rye straw, dung, axes, saws, augers and family members and neighbours. With no huge mortgage payments or escalating interest rates to deal with, the early immigrant could perhaps be envied.

Hand gristmill (*zhorna*), 1916, from east-central Alberta, for grinding grain.

Hardwood, stone, metal
93 x 84 x 43 cm
stick: 125 x 4 cm

CCFCS 73-764.1-41

Wardrobe, made in Buchanan, Saskatchewan, 1890–1900.

Painted pine
189.5 x 150.0 x 39.8 cm

CCFCS 81-139

(left)

Ukrainian immigrants filled trunks like this with the necessities of life for the first few years of pioneering on the Prairies. This particular example was brought to Canada in 1902 from western Ukraine and was probably used as a family storage chest for generations.

Painted wood
117 x 66 x 66 cm

CCFCS 79-773

(below)

Bench, 20th century, collected in Saskatchewan.

Wood
212 x 75 x 35 cm

CCFCS 78-320

Escape your heritage?

Never. It goes where you go; it sleeps where you sleep. No matter how often you brush your teeth, the memory stays in your mouth. No matter how often you wash your hands, it's there— ingrained in every pore of your body and spirit.

— Maara Lazechko Haas, 1977

Such traditional homes survived into the 1920s. They were then replaced by houses made with costly plank siding, which was flimsier than the log walls. The modern dwellings were often poorly insulated, badly designed, shoddily constructed and costlier than a traditional house.

Villages on the Prairies had to comply with a standard plan prepared by the railway companies. A station and grain elevators were constructed near the intersection of the main street and the railroad tracks. All signs were in English as was the village name, though its residents might speak

Bandura, 1962, made in Grimsby, Ontario.

Various woods, metal strings
140.0 x 48.8 x 9.0 cm

CCFCS 75-1366

Ukrainian. Only beyond the rail lines did Ukrainian names appear for villages and post offices. Within these bloc settlements of pioneering immigrants, each family lived on its own quarter-section in lonely isolation, punctuated by cold winters, hot summers, autumn fires, and spring mud. Many traditional practices disappeared in these rural enclaves, sometimes only because the men had to leave the farm to work for wages. In their absence, the women milked the cows and bypassed, for example, the ancient rituals which had men begin milking with a prayer to assure a good supply of milk. Similarly, traditional healers, who in Ukraine walked around a house and smaller villages to stave off disease, found it impossible to do this in Canada, given the greatly increased distances.

The Ukrainian pioneers were skilled in making and using many tools, especially farm implements. They fashioned harrows, ploughs, sickles, handmills and mortars for the production and processing of wheat. But it was from the braided dough, the final step in this chain of know-how, that distinctive, ethnic products were created. Similarly, it was not so much the growing and processing of flax to produce thread and cloth that was Ukrainian. Even as the thread went to looms to make cloth, there was still no ethnic aura. Not until the cloth was sewn into traditional forms and embroidered could it become *nashe* (ours).

Some products were more ethnically meaningful than others. Homemade music-makers, like the *tsymbaly*, played

Tsymbaly with playing sticks, 20th century, from Manitoba.

Wood with painted floral motifs, metal strings
122.0 x 37.5 x 12.8 cm

CCFCS 73-644

Ivan Semeniuk plays the *tsymbaly*, or hammered dulcimer, in Mundare, Alberta, July 1965.

CMC 85-3569

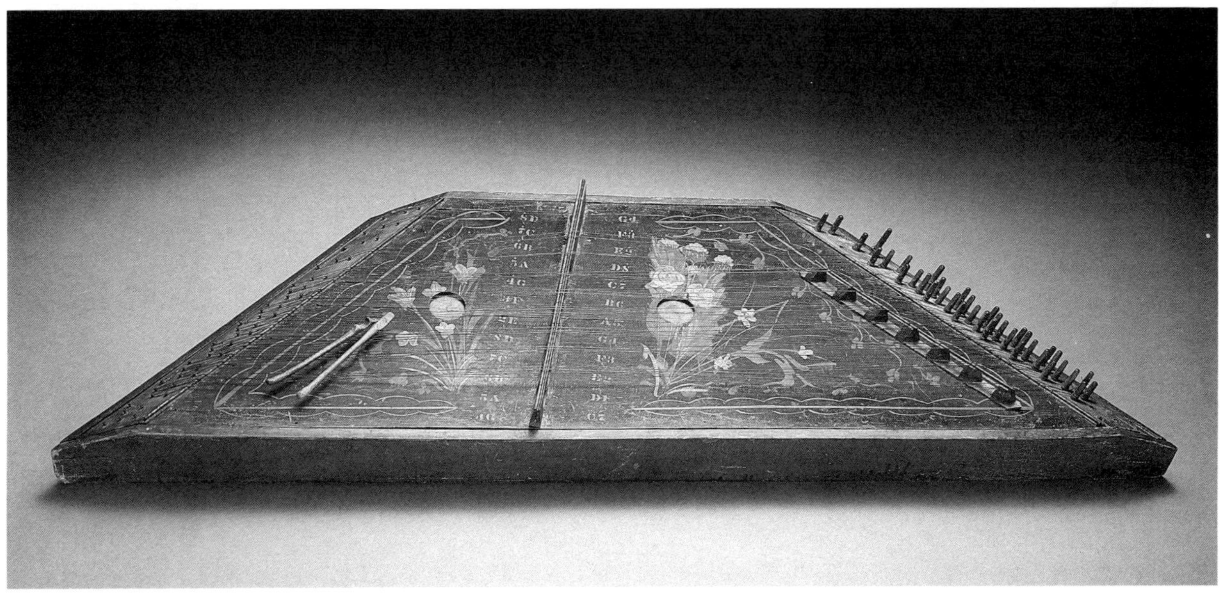

at old-time socials, and the lute-like *bandura*, once strummed by blind minstrels, are *nashe*. *Tsymbaly* were often brought to Canada by Ukrainian immigrants. They were also easy to make. Strings were stretched on a trapezoid wooden frame at a fixed tension to run over and under two bridges, forming three raised rows of strings. These were then struck with wooden sticks (*palychky* or *kistky*). The *bandura*, sometimes called the harp of the Ukrainians, is the national musical instrument of Ukraine. Thought to have originated in the Far East, this plucked, stringed instrument typically has a pear-shaped body. Short melody strings stretch over the upper right side of the resonance box; long base strings over the neck. From seven to thirty strings are tuned according to a diatonic scale. Its recent revival among youth in Canada can be traced to *bandura* musicians who immigrated to North America after the Second World War.

Canada's first Ukrainians viewed this country as a land of opportunity. Much of their material culture was left behind in Ukraine or did not survive in the new land; of the items that remain many serve mainly as ethnic symbols. The vitality of Ukrainian culture is still manifested in the church architecture, in traditional clothing such as the elaborately embroidered shirts, and in popular Ukrainian cuisine. This living culture also serves to remind us of the many talents brought to this country by Canada's Ukrainian pioneer immigrants.

What I listen to the most is the radio in my car....driving down the road in the middle of the Canadian prairie...When they have the Ukrainian hour, it's polka heaven. It's quite a lot of inspiration.

—K. D. Lang, 1989

Stefan Pidsosny, 1906–1977
"O My Sheep" circa 1970

Wall plaque in frame
Carved and painted wood
45 x 44 cm

CCFCS 71-774

Suggested Readings and Works Cited

Balan, Jars. *Salt and Braided Bread: Ukrainian Life in Canada*. Toronto: Oxford University Press, 1984.

Barnes, Susan J., and Walter S. Melion, eds. *Cultural Differentiation and Cultural Identity in the Visual Arts*. Washington: National Gallery of Art, 1989.

Berton, Pierre. *The Promised Land: Settling the West 1896–1914*. Toronto: McClelland and Stewart, 1970.

Bringéus, Nils-Arvid, ed. *Man and Picture: Papers from the First International Symposium for Ethnological Picture Research in Lund 1984*. Stockholm: Almqvist and Wiksell International, 1986.

Canadian Museum of Civilization. *The Ukrainians in Canada 1891–1991*. Theme issue of *Material History Bulletin* 29 (Spring 1989).

Cook, Ramsay. "William Kurelek: A Prairie Boy's Visions." *Journal of Ukrainian Studies* 5, no. 1 (Spring 1980): 33–48.

Encyclopedia of Ukraine. 2 vols. to date. Toronto: University of Toronto Press, 1984–.

Fischer, Michael M. J. "Ethnicity and the Post-Modern Arts of Memory." In *Writing Culture: The Poetics and Politics of Ethnography*, edited by James Clifford and George E. Marcus, pp. 194–233. Berkeley, Calif.: University of California Press, Berkeley, 1986.

Isajiw, Wsevolod W. "Definitions of Ethnicity." *Ethnicity* 1, no. 2 (1974): 111–124.

Jones, Michael Owen. *Exploring Folk Art: Twenty Years of Thought on Craft, Work and Aesthetics*. Ann Arbor Mich.: UMI Research Press, 1987.

Klymasz, Robert B. "Framing the Heritage: Towards an Understanding of the Ukrainian Arts in Canada." In *Millennium of Christianity in Ukraine, 988–1988,* edited by Oleh W. Gerus and Alexander Baran, pp. 293–95. Winnipeg: Ukrainian Academy of Arts and Sciences in Canada, 1989.

Kubijovyc, Volodymyr, ed. *Ukraine: A Concise Encyclopedia.* 2 vols. Toronto: University of Toronto Press, 1963–71.

Kurelek, William. "The Development of Ethnic Consciousness in a Canadian Artist." In *Identities: The Impact of Ethnicity on Canadian Society,* edited by W.W. Isajiw, pp. 46–56. Toronto: Peter Martin Associated Ltd., 1977.

Luciuk, Lubomyr Y., and Bohdan S. Kordan. *Creating a Landscape: A Geography of Ukrainians in Canada.* Maps by Geoffrey J. Matthews. Toronto: University of Toronto Press, 1989.

Lupul, Manoly R., ed. *A Heritage in Transition: Essays in the History of Ukrainians in Canada.* Toronto: McLelland and Stewart, 1982.

Lupul, Manoly R., ed. *Visible Symbols: Cultural Expression among Canada's Ukrainians.* Edmonton: Canadian Institute of Ukrainian Studies, University of Alberta, 1984.

Marunchak, Michael H. *The Ukrainian Canadians: A History.* 2nd ed. rev. Winnipeg and Ottawa: Ukrainian Free Academy of Sciences, 1982.

Roy, Gabrielle. "Little Ukraine." In *The Fragile Lights of Earth: Articles and Memories 1942–1970,* pp. 75–85. Translated by Alan Brown. Toronto: McClelland and Stewart, 1982.

Ukrainian Community Development Committee, Prairie Region. *Building the Future: Ukrainian Canadians in the 21st Century, A Blueprint For Action.* Edmonton: Ukrainian Community Development Committee, Prairie Region, 1986.

About the Contributors

Wsevolod W. Isajiw is Professor of Sociology, University of Toronto. He has published widely on topics relating to ethnicity and is one of Canada's leading authorities in the field. Currently Dr. Isajiw is researching ethnic identity retention.

Michael Owen Jones is Professor of History and Folklore and Director of the Center for the Study of Comparative Folklore and Mythology at the University of California, Los Angeles. A Fellow of the American Folklore Society, Dr. Jones has published several books and over sixty articles and review essays on such topics as faith healing, foodways, folk art and organizational folklore.

Robert B. Klymasz is Curator, East European Programme, Canadian Centre for Folk Culture Studies, Canadian Museum of Civilization. In a career that has spanned nearly thirty years, Dr. Klymasz has published extensively on Ukrainian folk traditions in Canada and has provided curatorial research and direction for several exhibitions.

Zenon S. Pohorecky is Professor of Anthropology and Archaeology, University of Saskatchewan, Saskatoon. Born in Galicia, Ukraine, and raised in western Canada, Dr. Pohorecky has an intimate knowledge of immigrant folkways on the Prairies.

Dmytro V. Stepovyk is Senior Researcher specializing in Ukrainian Art History with the M. Rylsky Institute of Art, Folklore and Ethnography, Ukrainian Academy of Sciences, in Kiev, Ukraine. Over a period of several months during 1988–89, Dr. Stepovyk was in Canada as a visiting professor and lectured across Canada at various universities.

Frances Swyripa is currently the recipient of a three-year research fellowship from the Social Sciences and Humanities Research Council of Canada, which she will hold at the Department of History, University of Alberta, Edmonton. Dr. Swyripa was also awarded another fellowship on the basis of her dissertation, "From Princess Olha to Baba: Images, Roles and Myths of the History of Ukrainian Women in Canada."

ARTISTS AND ARTISANS – AN AFTERWORD

One of the aims of this volume is to demonstrate the links between ethnicity and visual art as illustrated by the Ukrainian experience in Canada. Works by the following artists and artisans were instrumental in this regard, and for the record, we wish to document their participation in this process. All of them were represented in the exhibition **Art and Ethnicity: The Ukrainian Tradition in Canada**, as first shown at the Canadian Museum of Civilization in Hull, Quebec, August 1991 to February 1993. An asterisk (*) is used if work by the artist or artisan appears as an illustration in this book. Dates and place of residence are given, if known.

Allsopp, Judy, b. 1943, Winnipeg, Manitoba

Andruschak, Olga, 1921–1976, Saskatoon, Saskatchewan

Antonovych, Kateryna, 1884–1975, Winnipeg, Manitoba

Balan, Jars, b. 1952, Edmonton, Alberta

*Balas, Shawna, b. 1961, Winnipeg, Manitoba

*Bodnar, Nicholas, b. 1914, Edmonton, Alberta

*Bykowski, Liz, b. 1941, Edmonton, Alberta

Checkwitch, Robert, Manitoba

Cmoc, Bohdanna, b. 1948, Ottawa, Ontario

Czernicki, Stefan, b. 1946, Calgary, Alberta

*Demeda, Paul, b. 1960, Toronto, Ontario

Dolinsky, Vicky H., b. 1925, Flin Flon, Manitoba

Dutka, Frances, b. 1929, Grosse Isle, Manitoba

Farkavec, Dmytro, b. 1942, Winnipeg, Manitoba

Field, Saul, 1912–1987, Toronto, Ontario

Genush, Luba, b. 1924, Montréal, Quebec

Gretchyn, William, b. 1910, Winnipeg, Manitoba

Harasymchuk, Tillie, b. 1920, Thunder Bay, Ontario
*Harbuz, Ann, 1908–1989, North Battleford, Saskatchewan
Hrytzak, Isadore F., 1907–1983, Saskatchewan
*Husar, Natalka, b. 1951, Toronto, Ontario
Isajiw, Sophia, b. 1964, Toronto, Ontario
Iwanec, Parasia, b. ca. 1920, St. Catharines, Ontario
*Jaworski, Elizabeth, b. 1937, Toronto, Ontario
Johnson, Lindsay, b. ca. 1940, Dauphin, Manitoba
Karsh, Yousuf, b. 1908, Ottawa, Ontario
Kasijan, Vasyl', 1896–1976, Ukraine
Kereliuk, Adele, b. 1926, Toronto, Ontario
Kinasevych, Orest, b. 1962, Vancouver, British Columbia
Klym, George, California
Kolesar, Julijan, b. 1927, Montréal, Quebec
Kornavitch-Tomlinson, Olga, b. 1929, Lone Butte, British Columbia
Kost, Robert, b. 1936, Lac du Bonnet, Manitoba
Kostiuk, Lena, b. 1930, Edmonton, Alberta
Koszarycz, Halyna, b. 1931, Edmonton, Alberta
Kotyk, Cheryl, b. 1950, Arran, Saskatchewan
Kowal, Roman, b. 1922, Winnipeg, Manitoba
*Kuc, Chester, b. 1931, Edmonton, Alberta
Kuch, Peter, 1917–1980, Winnipeg, Manitoba
Kulyk, Alice, b. 1952, Winnipeg, Manitoba
*Kurelek, William, 1927–1977, Toronto, Ontario
*Lada, Sophia, b. 1941, Toronto, Ontario
*Lenhardt, Molly, b. 1920, Melville, Saskatchewan
Levytsky, Myron, b. 1913, Toronto, Ontario
Lipinski, Peter, 1888–1975, Edmonton, Alberta
Lobchuk, William, b. 1942, Winnipeg, Manitoba
Logush, Ruslan, b. 1950, Montréal, Quebec
*Lopata, Pavlo, b. 1945, Toronto, Ontario
Lozowchuk, Anna, b. 1903, Hafford, Saskatchewan
Luchak, Karen, b. 1956, Winnipeg, Manitoba

Luhovy, Laryssa, b. 1942, Montréal, Quebec
Lysak, Adriana, b. 1930, Montréal, Quebec
Markowsky, Martha, Ottawa, Ontario
Maydanyk, Jacob, 1891–1984, Winnipeg, Manitoba
Mazepa, Wolodymyr, Rawdon, Quebec
Melnick, Steve, b. 1959, Sydney, Nova Scotia
Melnyk, Doug, b. 1952, Winnipeg, Manitoba
Michalesky, Bernard R. J., b. 1936, Winnipeg, Manitoba
*Miller, Shelagh, b. 1928, Grosse Isle, Manitoba
Mol, Leo, b. 1915, Winnipeg, Manitoba
*Mordowanec-Regenbogen, Halyna, b. 1945, Windsor, Ontario
Mudryj, Daria, b. 1952, Winnipeg, Manitoba
Mykytyshyn, Marcel, Saskatoon, Saskatchewan
Nosyk, Irene R., Toronto, Ontario
*Nykilchuk, Nick, b. 1931, Sudbury, Ontario
Ostafijchuk, Ivan, b. 1940, Toronto, Ontario
Parobec-Dzwonyk, Lillian, b. 1935, Kenora, Ontario
*Paskievich, John, b. 1947, Winnipeg, Manitoba
*Pesklivets, Nicholas, 1911–1988, Edmonton, Alberta
*Petelycky, Steven, b. 1923, Richmond, British Columbia
Phillips, Walter J., 1884–1963, Winnipeg, Manitoba
Pidruchney, Anna, 1909–1989, Vegreville, Alberta
*Pidsosny, Stefan, 1906-1977, Regina, Saskatchewan
Poitras Dugas, Louise, b. 1941, Rimouski, Quebec
Polujan, Alexandra, b. 1945, Vancouver, British Columbia
Proch, Don, b. 1944, Winnipeg, Manitoba
Pronko, Mary, b. 1924, Sydney, Nova Scotia
Robertson, Jeanine, Ottawa, Ontario
Sadlowski, Julian, b. 1936, North Battleford, Saskatchewan
Saprowich, Frank, b. 1939, Winnipeg, Manitoba
Sawka, Daria, b. 1923, Montréal, Quebec
*Schlieper, Heiko, b. 1931, Ottawa, Ontario
Semchishen, Orest, b. 1932, Edmonton, Alberta
Semotiuk, Zenovia, b. 1970, Winnipeg, Manitoba

Senkiw, Christina, b. 1950, Toronto, Ontario
Shackleton, Kathleen, Winnipeg, Manitoba
*Shewchuk, Jeanette, b. 1948, Warren, Manitoba
Shostak, Peter, b. 1943, Victoria, British Columbia
Simpson, Muriel, 1889–1963, Saskatoon, Saskatchewan
*Snihurowycz, Taras, b. 1918, Winnipeg, Manitoba
*Stefanchuk, William, Tolstoi, Manitoba
Stefaniuk, Maureen, b. 1953, Verigin, Saskatchewan
Stryjek, Dmytro, b. 1899, Saskatoon, Saskatchewan
Szulhan, Oksana, b. 1952, Vancouver, British Columbia
*Tascona, Tony, b. 1926, St. Boniface, Manitoba
*Temertey, Ludmilla, b. 1944, Toronto, Ontario
Tokaryk, John, 1913–1980, Ottawa, Ontario
Veito, Walter J., b. 1943, The Pas, Manitoba
Warbansky, Elizabeth, b. 1953, Winnipeg, Manitoba
*Wasylyshen, Ben, b. 1961, Winnipeg, Manitoba
*Wasylyshen, Eve, b. 1937, Winnipeg, Manitoba
*Wasylyshen, Ted, b. 1932, Winnipeg, Manitoba
Wellman, Loraine, b. 1936, Richmond, British Columbia
Wlasiuk, E., b. 1922, Oshawa, Ontario
Woods, Anna, b. 1947
Woychyshyn, Tony, Saskatchewan
Yaroslawski, Semen, 1899–1966, Sydney, Nova Scotia
Yarymowich, Anne, b. 1956, Toronto, Ontario
Young (Zahara), Vida, Detroit, Michigan
Yurchuk, Vera, b. 1941, Toronto, Ontario
Yuristy, Russell, b. 1936, Ottawa, Ontario
Yuzyk, Lucya Yarymowich, b. 1953, Ottawa, Ontario
Zaporzan, Shirley, b. 1937, Winnipeg, Manitoba

Robert B. Klymasz